A Dream
I Lived Alone

PRAISE FOR USTAD GHULAM MUSTAFA KHAN

'He has a positive attitude towards life and always wants to teach and share his knowledge. He rarely wants anything in return, which is the one great thing that I have learnt from him'—A.R. Rahman

'The one thing I find amazing and highly admirable in Ustadji is his patience and his capacity to give unconditional love to his students. He works very hard with every student and is genuinely desirous of imparting his knowledge to each one of them'—Waheeda Rehman

'What can I say about such a big artiste? Ustad Ghulam Mustafa Khan is a very big voice. He is an institution; he is a tradition. He is the Hindustan we seek these days. Hindustan, or for that matter any country, is not in its buildings, its walls, its mountains or its grasslands; it is in its manners, its culture and its art [. . .] it is with the artistes of the country. I salute Ustad Ghulam Mustafa Khan with full belief, faith and respect. He is the one sun who has shown so many the light of the stars. And we are fans of those stars who are his fans, which means that our relationship with him has transcended generations. I pray that he continues to shower his blessings on all of us and continues to spread his knowledge and music forever'—Javed Akhtar

'The one discipline that he always insists on is regular riyaz. He says, "Always do riyaz. Whatever you learn, practise it [. . .] If you just learn a song, it will stay in your head for some days and then you will forget it. Unless that song settles in your throat, your voice will not support it"'—Hariharan

'Whenever Ustad Ghulam Mustafa Khan's name is mentioned, a sense of peace envelops my heart and soul. A flash of light sparks in my mind. Khan sahib has dedicated his entire life to music. Not only has he set a benchmark of knowledge, he has also enlightened many students like me by blessing us. I am grateful to god that I was able to meet such a fine human being and learn music from him'—Sonu Nigam

'I always tell everyone that guruji not only teaches music, but also how to live one's life. He teaches you how to treat each other with respect, the importance of relationships and how to handle them. He teaches you how to be a good human being'—Shaan

'Khan sahib is like a father to me. I have learnt singing by listening to him on the radio and the television. For me, he is my school of music and will always stay so. Whoever he has trained have established themselves very well and made a name for themselves'—Anup Jalota

'I call him my *chacha* [uncle]. My father was a very good friend of Ustadji and regarded him as an elder brother. I am delighted to have had the opportunity of knowing such a pure, talented and good man. When people receive blessings from their gurus, it can change the course of their lives forever. Ustadji is one such guru'—Lalit Sen

'He is known more through his disciples than by himself'—Roop Kumar Rathod

'Not many, or very few, people know him the way I do. Besides learning music from him, I have learnt so much more that I can safely say that if it had not been for him, I would not have been in Mumbai today. Long ago when I had just landed in the city without any income or a roof over my head, Ustadji helped me out—not only did he get me a job but also helped me in many other ways. Thanks to him I could sustain and establish myself. Whatever I am today is only because of him. For me, he is no less than god himself'—Abhijeet Bhattacharya

USTAD GHULAM MUSTAFA KHAN

with NAMRATA GUPTA KHAN

A Dream
I Lived Alone

EBURY
PRESS

An imprint of Penguin Random House

EBURY PRESS

USA | Canada | UK | Ireland | Australia
New Zealand | India | South Africa | China | Singapore

Ebury Press is part of the Penguin Random House group of companies
whose addresses can be found at global.penguinrandomhouse.com

Published by Penguin Random House India Pvt. Ltd
4th Floor, Capital Tower 1, MG Road,
Gurugram 122 002, Haryana, India

First published in Ebury Press by Penguin Random House India 2018

10 9 8 7 6 5 4 3 2

The views and opinions expressed in this book are the authors' own and the
facts are as reported by them which have been verified to the extent possible,
and the publishers are not in any way liable for the same.

ISBN 9780670090860

Typeset in Adobe Caslon Pro by Manipal Digital Systems, Manipal

Printed at Replika Press Pvt. Ltd, India

www.penguin.co.in

This is a legitimate digitally printed version of the book and therefore might not
have certain extra finishing on the cover.

Ustad Ghulam Mustafa Khan:

To my father, Ustad Waris Hussain Khan sahib, and my gurus, Ustad Fida Hussain Khan sahib and Ustad Nissar Hussain Khan sahib. Also, with gratitude to all those who have helped me and been a part of my journey.

Namrata Gupta Khan:

To my entire Khan and Gupta families.

Contents

Award, Art and the Artiste   1

Tu Data Dayaani—God, You Are Merciful and Kind   15

The Rebel in Me   31

The Fifties—Early Years of My Independence   43

Bombay—My Karam Bhoomi   55

My Wife, My Humsafar   61

Music and Marriage in the Sixties   69

Children of the Sixties   93

The Seventies—and the Music Plays on   113

Children of the Seventies   127

My Elder Brother, My Ustad   145

My One-of-a-kind Mamu Sahib   149

When the Cold Weather Leads to Composition and
Other Stories   153

Through Cities, Concerts and Children Growing Up   161

Disciples and Teachers   167

Friends and Fans   177

Acknowledgements   199

THE RAMPUR – SAHASWAN GHARANA

Rooted In The Ancient Seniya Traditions As Initiated By

The Great Tansen

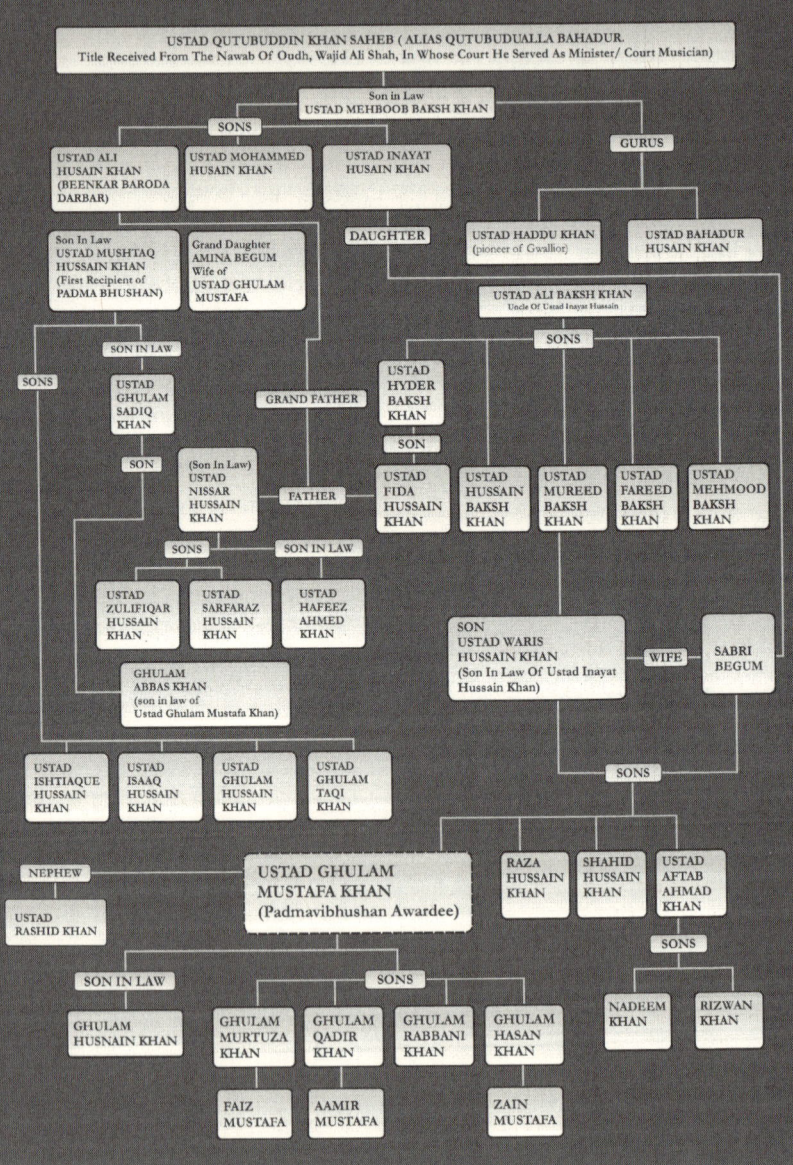

Award, Art and the Artiste

On 20 March 2018, I was one among the many invitees to the Padma Awards ceremony at the Rashtrapati Bhavan, home of the President of our country. I travelled there with my wife Amina, daughter-in-law Namrata, my sons Murtuza, Qadir, Rabbani and Hasan, and my grandsons Faiz and Aamir.

I waited, as did the other guests and invitees, for the names to be announced. Music composer Ilaiyaraaja, at the announcement of his name, walked across the red carpeted path with a swift and self-assured dignity to receive the Padma Vibhushan, one among three people this year to have been selected, the other two being renowned scholar, author and philosopher P. Parameswaran, and me, a classical musician and composer. Upon the announcement of my name, I walked the short distance across the floor to reach President Ram Nath Kovind and received the award from him on behalf of the music that, by the grace of God, chose me. Conscious of the many eyes, the camera lenses and the flashes of light that are a part of every event today, the President and I greeted each other with a 'Namaste' and a handshake. He pinned a medallion to my chest. I held out my hands as he handed me the *sanad*, the award certificate, and we turned to face the cameras for a moment, standing still, holding that award between us, a courtesy to the photographers; those seconds of stillness. This was at the Civil Investiture Ceremony of the Padma Awards, and I am now a Padma Vibhushan awardee.

The years pass swiftly. I have been to Rashtrapati Bhavan twice before—twenty-seven years ago, in 1991, for receiving the Padma Shri, and twelve years ago, in 2006, for receiving the Padma Bhushan. An interesting titbit—Rashtrapati Bhavan was formally inaugurated in 1931, and that is the year I was born. Of course, when I was born, I certainly had no consciousness of the possibility that sixty years into the future, I would be called upon to meet the then President of India, Shri Venkataraman, and receive the Padma Shri. Or that at the age of seventy-five, I would meet yet another President of India, A.P.J. Kalam, and receive the Padma Bhushan.

In fact, I was a child who began to speak quite late. I have no memory of this, but it is well-known family history that my parents, who come from an illustrious line of classical music composers, singers and teachers, were very apprehensive when I, their son, had not said a word till the age of two! I think that perhaps we are all constantly under construction. As the weeks and months turn into years and decades, we build and re-build, and we do this in our own way, at a uniquely individual pace. Not that this thought could allay the anxiety of my parents. I belonged to a family that followed the Rampur-Sahaswan gharana of Hindustani classical music. It was only natural that I carried on the family tradition and enrich the legacy of my ancestors.

My father, Ustad Waris Hussain Khan, was the grandson of Ustad Qutubuddin Khan, and the son-in-law of the famous vocalist Ustad Inayat Hussain Khan. Ustad Qutubuddin Khan sahib, celebrated *beenkar* and exponent of khayal and dhrupad, was a musician at the court of Nawab Wajid Ali Shah of Awadh. Ustad Inayat Hussain Khan, my grandfather, was the founder of the Rampur-Sahaswan gharana. He was married to the daughter of Ustad Haddu Khan, the pioneer of the Gwalior gharana. Their family traced their Senia traditions to *mian* Tansen from the darbar of Akbar. My dear mother, whom I call Ammi, daughter of Ustad Inayat Hussain Khan, shared and understood the sense of responsibility and expectation around a child born to this artistic inheritance.

Ustad Waris Hussain Khan was a worried and concerned man because his son could not utter a word. He did not despair or give up hope, though. Many elders in the family have told me that instead of giving up hope or blaming his luck, my father decided to be proactive. I believe he used to put me on his chest, face downwards and sing so that I would imitate him and try to sing along. Well, I could not sing, but my mother told me that I used to enjoy his singing and coax out some 'Yayaya' sounds of my own as accompaniment. This was a source of great relief for my parents, as they felt assured that there was nothing wrong with my vocal cords. My father continued to work on me in a similar fashion as he believed that if I exerted myself to bring out sounds, lying on my stomach, it would strengthen my vocal cords as well as 'open up' my lungs.

I think his remedy worked because soon afterwards, I uttered my first words and gradually started speaking like other children of my age. My parents were delighted and promptly started my classical music training in earnest. Though I could not understand the words at that young age, I could remember the tune and the grammar of what was being taught to me.

As a child, I learnt many lessons from my gurus and I remember one that stays with me until today. I was doing my *riyaz* one day when my guru, Ustad Nissar Khan sahib, walked into the room. When he saw me, he asked me to stop and sing in front of the mirror so that I could see the faces I was making while singing! He told me to control my expressions and never contort my face while singing. He told me that when I sing, it should appear effortless. I took his advice and regularly practised in front of the mirror to ensure that I never again made faces while singing, and I am deeply grateful to him for giving me this advice, which I have the privilege of passing on here.

The life of an artiste, as I have always heard and known of it, is a life dedicated to the practice and performance of your art with all your spirit and soul. The house I grew up in was a big one, and life with my family at home was about responsibility and riyaz. 'Riyaz' is the Urdu word for 'practice'. It is my commitment to my music, and this, more than any other word, to those who have been my students, remains the most important and strongest aspect of my teaching. It sums up my life.

Did I dream of awards and rewards? Well, no. The earliest of my dreams that I do remember, and it was truly a fantastical dream, was that one day, people would listen to me on All India Radio. When I was a child, radio was not a common part of every household. All India Radio is just a year older than me,[1] having begun as a government takeover of radio operations in 1930, but at the time, it was the Indian State Broadcasting Service. It was renamed All India Radio a few years later. It was when I first heard my uncle and guru, Ustad Fida Hussain Khan sahib, and later my cousin and my guru, Ustad Nissar Hussain Khan sahib and Ustad Mushtaq Hussain Khan sahib, on All India Radio, that I too aspired to achieve this feat. Radio has played an important part in my story.

The world was very small when I was young. There was no media like TV or radio through which I could be exposed to music from the other gharanas. I only heard and learnt about my gharana from my elders.

Whenever I did riyaz, I made sure that no one came to know about it. I used to hide it from everyone, thinking that someone's evil eye would befall me. I never thought about whether people would love or not love my voice and my singing. Instead, I always sang as if I were worshipping the ability to sing. It is when people actually started to appreciate my voice that I realized that music removes barriers and that people, in fact, feel peace and derive comfort from listening to my songs.

Namrata, more my daughter than a daughter-in-law, is the reason I share my dreams and stories in these pages. I

---

[1] http://allindiaradio.gov.in/Profile/Growth%20and%20 Development/Pages/default.aspx

am a musician, a composer, a singer, a teacher. I am not a writer. Yet, there is this feeling I have lived with, and perhaps ignored for these many decades, that my gurus and teachers, my family, my dear wife, who is my true humsafar, my children—they have supported me more than I have been able to acknowledge. Therefore, in the lesser known stories of my life, I wish to profess my gratitude for the gifts, the love and the blessings I have received.

I believe that all honour and awards go to the art; I am just a medium.

Alhamdulillah

All praise is due to God alone.

My name is Namrata Gupta Khan.

I belong to an educated, middle-class family. I grew up as part of a small nuclear family, just five of us—my mom and my dad, my two younger brothers and me. A strong work ethic had been inculcated in us from a young age. My brothers and I were raised in an atmosphere where each of us knew we would grow up to shoulder responsibilities and stand on our own two feet. My mom is a hard-working homemaker, my dad is a criminal lawyer, one of my brothers is a telecom engineer and the other is a civil and corporate lawyer.

I started working at the age of sixteen. I was studying in college while also employed when a friend of mine told me that she wanted me to 'meet someone'. Even though I was a sociable person and an extrovert, I was also a bit reserved when I met new people. I declined my friend's proposal, knowing what 'meet someone' meant. She was trying to set me up with someone, but I was simply not interested in doing all that till I had found my feet and my independence and had been able to contribute something to the family that meant so much to me. My friend did not give up, but wheedled, coaxed, and continued her entreaties that I should meet this 'someone'. Finally, she wore me down and I agreed.

The 'someone' I met happened to be Rabbani.

You might find it strange, but that was the only introduction I had of him. No second name or any other information about him. Odd though it may seem, even to me when I think back upon those days, the thought never struck me. I liked the man and that was enough for me. I never wanted to know what his unique name meant, who he was, and what his family background was at all.

Rabbani was not in college with me, but he would come to meet me every day. He used to wait for me outside the college and we began spending time together. Gradually, we became good friends. I trusted the great degree of comfort I felt with him and found him to be highly respectful and caring.

Six months flew by and then, one day, Rabbani proposed to me. I hesitated for a moment, but then accepted his proposal happily. I knew he was already a core part of my life.

I was happy and excited and decided to share the news with the friend who had introduced me to him. It was then that she told me the meaning of his name and that he was a Muslim.

This revelation made no difference to me, but when I told my mother about him, she was shocked to hear that I had chosen a Muslim for my life partner. She vehemently objected to our relationship. My telling her that Rabbani was a wonderful human being, and that his religion made no difference to our love for each other, did not pacify or convince her. She told Dad and both of them were quite upset that I had fallen in love with a Muslim. I did not blame them because I understood their concerns. I knew they were both liberal and secular, but to have their daughter marry into a different religion, with its different customs and norms, was very hard for them to accept.

Well, to cut a long story short, though Rabbani and I were disappointed and upset at the opposition of my parents, we decided to honour my parent's wishes. We decided that we would get married when we had their blessings. We promised each other that if we could not marry each other, we would not marry at all.

I do not really know if Rabbani ever broached this subject with his family. Perhaps he did not, because he later told me that when, even at the great insistence of his family and elders, he refused to get married, an elderly woman in his family, out of love and concern for him, inquired about his sexual orientation and preference. He calmed her down and told her that he would get married when the time was right for him to do so or when he found a girl he actually wished to spend the rest of his life with.

Time passed, and our relationship matured. We were both growing up together and loved spending time together. There were days when we would both despair at thoughts of the future, but the fact that we were together carried us through those difficult times.

I finished my studies and took up a job, which kept me busy. Rabbani followed his musical inclinations and talent. He was also running an event management company that organized shows across India and the world.

Twelve long years passed like this.

Over time, I noticed that my parents' opposition to our union was not as vehement as it used to be. They had met Rabbani and quite liked him as a person. It was only the religious and cultural differences that kept them from accepting him completely.

As these things did not matter to me, I never actually asked Rabbani about his family background. I only knew that his father was a classical vocalist.

Then, one fine day, after our long and trying ordeal, the sun shone on us when Rabbani's parents came to my house with the proposal of marriage.

My mother was suddenly, totally overwhelmed. She started crying when Rabbani's father, Ustad Ghulam Mustafa Khan, told my parents, in his inimitable and endearing way, 'Hamari bahu hamari beti hai. Namrata hamari beti hai jo aap ke ghar mein pal rahi thi, isliye hum apni beti aap se maangne aaye hain (For us, our daughter-in-law is our daughter. Namrata is our daughter, whom you have raised in your house, but now we have come to ask your permission to take her with us).'

That was it. Just those few words and life was beautiful, bright and cheerful once again.

I will never know if my parents ever regretted their decision to oppose our match since I never asked them about it. I was only thankful that everything was suddenly sorted out and before I knew it, a date was fixed for our marriage. Rabbani and I had never allowed ourselves to become bitter and for us, it was an 'all's well that ends well' situation.

Rabbani and I got married on 12. 12. 2012 in Mumbai, with the blessings of both our families. My in-laws welcomed me into their hearts and their home with great affection and love. I was ecstatic and thanked God over many silent prayers.

This is the story of how I got married into a large joint family of sixteen members—Papa, Ammi, their four sons and their wives and then their children. I will admit that I did feel a little anxious about how I was going to adjust to a different culture, a different way of doing things, a lifestyle and routines I knew very little about.

When I got married, I only knew that Papa was a celebrated Hindustani classical singer. What I did not know was that this affectionate person, whom I call Papa, who spends hours chatting with me and indulges us all with his love and care, is a doyen of classical music in India, loved, respected and celebrated nationally and internationally.

I soon realized that artistes and singers, who are celebrities, often visited our house to meet and pay their respects to my father-in-law. I thought that it was because of his age and experience. What I did not know was that many of these familiar visitors, such as Sonu Nigam, A.R. Rahman, Hariharan, Shaan and others were actually his disciples and called him 'Guruji' (teacher).

I was curious to know more about him, but whenever I asked him to tell me more about himself, he would give me a gentle smile and stay silent. It was then that I decided to ask Rabbani, and do some research on my own. What I discovered left me completely awestruck.

My god, this man is a living legend!

Now I felt a new pressure, of my role and the possible expectations from that role in maintaining the brand, the pressure of the tagline that was now mine—daughter-in-law of Ustad Ghulam Mustafa Khan. I struggled with these thoughts and feelings, but for a very short period. I soon realized that the fears and apprehensions were of my own making, for no one in the family put any pressure on me. So I settled back into a state of comfort with my new situation. I began to find myself increasingly curious and interested in finding out more about the person, the brand that is Ustad Ghulam Mustafa Khan.

Recently, at his eighty-seventh birthday celebrations, hosted by his dear disciple and the man with a golden voice, Sonu Nigam, many known names in music from the Indian film industry were present to pay their tribute to him. At this gathering, the famous poet, lyricist and screenplay writer Javed Akhtar sahib perfectly captured in a few words what sixty thousand words cannot convey as well!

He said, 'Hum jin sitaron ke fan hain, woh sab Ustad Ghulam Mustafa Khan ke fan hain (the stars whom we are fans of are all fans of Ustad Ghulam Mustafa Khan).'

As the co-writer of this autobiography, A Dream I Lived Alone, I play the part of a 'sutradhar'. Over many conversations across five years with Papa, I have listened to his stories and recollections carefully, and made notes of my own, based on the questions that I have asked him and others in the family, as well as students and others. Most of what you will read in this autobiography is based on my understanding and translation of his words as he shared his stories and his memories with me.

It has not been easy to make him speak about his laurels because he does not like to dwell on his achievements. I have insisted, entreated and sometimes pushed his indulgence to bully him a little and make him speak of his amazing journey so far.

Recently, as I watched him being honoured with the second highest civilian honour, the Padma Vibhushan, and receive his award from the President of India, Honourable Ram Nath Kovind ji, I was overwhelmed by the images that came to my mind. My heart was full, as were my eyes with sudden tears; I think I stopped breathing for a moment.

The years rolled back.

I saw a boy running to do his riyaz after wrapping two chapattis for a lunch with himself and an audience of nobody.

I saw a child just eight years old, holding his breath with anxious excitement, waiting for his name to be announced before he stepped out in front of his first public audience.

I saw a son gripping the hand of his mother, as she lay ill and he wept not knowing what he could do for her.

I saw a young man who sang before music maestros whose very names are spoken of in hushed tones of reverence. Ustad Bade Ghulam Ali Khan sahib. Ustad Amir Khan sahib. He was blessed by these greats and thereafter, became one in his own right.

I saw a husband standing in a Bandra doorway, the monsoon rain pouring down upon him as he raises his hand to ring the bell, surprise his wife and eat hot pakoras.

I saw a father trotting on all fours, playing horse with his daughter clinging to his back and shouting with joy.

I saw this man, walking back with his award scroll amid the loud applause from the who's who of the country in the Ashok Hall in the President's house in New Delhi.

'Wah, ustad, wah!' I may have said this aloud. How beautiful it is to live with someone who has been breathing music all his life.

Before you read on, I would like to quote something he has said that you will find in the pages ahead:

'*Every artiste's path is unique. Hearing another person's story of success can be motivating, but your story is your own.*'

This is the story of *Padma Vibhushan Ustad Ghulam Mustafa Khan.*

Tu Data Dayaani—God, You Are Merciful and Kind

I was born on 3 March 1931 in Badaun, Uttar Pradesh, the eldest son in a family of four brothers and three sisters. My father, Ustad Waris Hussain Khan sahib, was the son of Ustad Mureed Baksh, who was a great musician. My mother, Sabri Begum, was the daughter of the founder of the Rampur-Sahaswan gharana of music, Ustad Inayat Hussain Khan sahib. Ustad Inayat Hussain Khan sahib was one of the three sons of Ustad Mehboob Khan sahib, who was a singer and musician at the court of the Nawab of Rampur in Uttar Pradesh. He was a beenkar, one who plays the veena. I do remember hearing this story somewhere about one of the children, Ustad Inayat Khan sahib's brother, Ali Hussain Khan, that he had arms of unusually great length and that a special *been* was made for him to play music. Later, he was sent to Baroda, where he became a beenkar at the royal court.

Many people are probably unfamiliar with the rich musical heritage and traditions of our country. I take this opportunity to document the Rampur-Sahaswan gharana, whose music roots can be traced back to the sixteenth century, to the great, respected Tansen sahib. This connection is drawn from one of his direct descendants,

15

Bahadur Hussain Khan sahib, who I think was his great-grandson. These stories are centuries old and I cannot confirm the authenticity of their origins, but as it is with family lineages, most of the records are oral and remain so. All of Tansen sahib's children were musicians. He is a great and indelible part of the story of the music of Hindustan. Everyone knows of him as one of the Navratnas at the court of Akbar. He was born in Gwalior and spent most of his life at the court of the Raja of Rewa, Ramchandra Singh. There are many legends surrounding Tansen sahib, the most well-known being the story that when he sang Raag Deepak, flames sprang up and spread by themselves, lighting diyas. Another was that he could cause rain to fall by singing Raag Megh Malhar. I grew up hearing these mesmerizing stories and various versions of them.

Bahadur Hussain Khan sahib, Tansen's descendant, if the stories are to be believed, was a court musician in Rampur. He was guru to Inayat Hussain sahib, as well as a friend of my great-grandfather, Ustad Qutubuddin Khan sahib. Music families and music traditions are passed on from the great gurus to their disciples. Often, from such inheritance is born the singer, the musician, the one who keeps the tradition alive and brings to it his own particular spirit and practice. Inayat Hussain sahib married the daughter of Ustad Haddu Khan sahib of the Gwalior gharana, who became his guru as well. Thus, unfolds our story of the Rampur-Sahaswan gharana, born of Senia traditions, going back to mian Tansen and his music!

The speciality of our gharana is voice culture. Some *bandishe* (compositions) and different, special training are involved, so that the range and level of voice increases. We also work on the pronunciation of words.

My father was a great vocalist himself, but he fulfilled his dreams through me and gave up everything to make me all that I am today. Whatever I have achieved, all that I have learnt, is all because of his sacrifice, commitment, love and blessings. After my father had begun my initiation to music and given me my basic classical music training, he sent me off to learn more from his cousin, Ustad Fida Hussain Khan sahib, who was a court musician at the Baroda royal darbar. Ustad Fida Hussain Khan's father, Ustad Haider Khan sahib, learnt music from his cousin, Ustad Inayat Hussain Khan sahib. I later studied music under my cousin, Ustad Nissar Hussain Khan sahib, son of Ustad Fida Hussain sahib, who, as a child, was taught by his grandfather.

Ustad Nissar Hussain Khan sahib is known to the world for his marvellous Kangan Mudaria in Raag Multani. Superfast metre, extraordinary tunes, matchless rendition of compositions—these are what he excelled at. It has been said by some of the greats of music that he is the chosen one of Allah to sing taranas. He represented the Rampur darbar and performed at a programme organized by King George V, which also led to his becoming the court musician of Baroda at the young age of eleven at the personal recommendation of King George V.

I consider Ustad Nissar Khan sahib as my respected guru. I remember when we had gone to Jaipur for a show in the early eighties, he jokingly told me that if someone asked him about the compositions that I was creating in his name and style, he would not know what to say. I told him in a light-hearted manner that if he wanted, I could teach all the compositions (bandishes) to his other disciples and then forget them myself. When he heard this, he burst out laughing.

It was also upon the advice of my guru that I learnt light and semi-classical forms such as thumri, dadra, kajri, the poetic forms of the geet and the ghazal, and spiritual forms including bhajans, besides the classical forms of composition, dhrupad and khayal. All that I have heard, all that I have learnt over the years tells me that music itself is a book and all the different types of music are chapters of this same book. Just listening, by itself, is a part of the learning process. I am ever grateful to my gurus because of the wide and varied introduction, appreciation and training in these various forms of music. This has helped me keep an open mind.

Once, I was travelling with some other musicians and an actor in a car when suddenly, the music being played caught my attention. I had never heard this style before and later learnt that it was some Spanish instrumental music. I was identifying the notes and enjoying the way the composition progressed. I could not help myself—I started vocalizing the sargam. Strange, is it? To imagine the Hindustani classical filter interpreting Spanish instrumental? I knew from the expressions of my companions that they were quite astonished. Yet, as I continued, they could feel it too, that music, as I felt it! They began to nod their heads and smile at my improvisations. I believe that is the way of music. If you are musical in your soul, then no music is a stranger. I listen to all kinds of music. Different kinds of music are like different flowers in one garden—when you wander, you see and feel that each flower has its own fragrance and colour, each is distinct, and each is unique.

I have had the honour of singing before many audiences in India and across the world, of recording songs in studios, for radio, films and documentaries. I will always remember my first opportunity to perform at a concert. It was the custom then that on Janmashtami, those interested in music would give their debut public performance during the festival. Ali Maqsood, the chairperson of the municipality, organized the Janmashtami function in Badaun each year, and year, he gave me the opportunity to perform. So it was in the Victoria Garden (now known as Gandhi Maidan) in Badaun, that I gave a performance before a public audience for the first time in my life. The year was 1939 and I was eight years old. I do not remember how I felt. It was a long time ago. I know that I sang, and I know that people said I sang well.

Life did not change much after this as my father made sure none of it ever went to my head. He was very particular about me practising my music. Whenever he used to step out of the house, he used to instruct the neighbours to keep an eye on me, and if they found me outside the house when it was not my playtime, they were to send me home to do riyaz and also report me to my father. As it turned out, my neighbours were extra conscientious and would send me back inside whenever they saw me. My father would then scold me for not taking my singing seriously.

Once, a neighbour came home and asked me to sing for him. I did so, and after I had finished, he praised me a great deal. My father, who was present, got upset with the neighbour and immediately scolded me in front of him. He also tapped me on the head to let me know that praise should not make me feel complacent.

'You will spoil my son if you heap false praise on him,' he told the surprised neighbour and asked me to practise harder to master the nuances of music. He went on to make my practice schedule even stricter.

As I remember and record these stories from my past, I feel a stronger sense of being indebted to my grandparents, my parents and my neighbours for their contribution in making me a singer. Not that my neighbours were always going to be so supportive in the years to come! I have seen and experienced all sides of these relationships of life. As a child, my neighbours loved and encouraged me. However, it was not so later! More of those stories in time.

The result of all this discipline and strictness from all quarters is that I practised for eight to twelve hours daily to master my art. I was always singing; it was my passion. I grew up dedicating my life to music.

When I fell ill with a severe bout of cough, fever and body ache, the reader can well imagine my plight. I was about nine years old. Just about a year had passed since my first public performance. Riyaz became impossible. I experienced a lot of chest pain and difficulty in breathing. Of course, my parents were worried about my condition, and because I was in that state, I was unable to practise singing. A doctor was called in. His diagnosis was pneumonia. A list of medicines was prescribed. Alongside this, a second list was made—of foods I was not allowed to eat. As far as I can recall, it included everything I liked eating! The doctor actually told my parents to feed me as little as possible so that the bacteria does not get nutrition and multiply. Therefore, not only could I no longer do my riyaz, but I remained hungry and felt deeply deprived.

One day, when the tough regimen became too much, and pangs of hunger overcame me, I, finding nothing else to eat in the house at that particular time, picked up a barni (pickle jar) and ate all the mango pickle that was in it. I stuck my head under a pillow so nobody could see what I was doing and polished off that entire jar. When my mother found out, she was both shocked and disbelieving of my feat! How could a nine-year-old boy, coughing and wheezing, sick with pneumonia, eat up a whole jar of pickle? What a scolding I received! I am very far from being nine years old today, but I can still hear her voice in my ears.

Surprisingly, instead of having an adverse effect, I think the pickle helped me get better and soon, I recovered from the pneumonia. Of course, I would not advise anybody else suffering from pneumonia to do what I did!

I never had pneumonia again in my life. I have never had pickle again in my life either!

In fact, I did some things as a child that I have never again repeated in my life. I suppose this is true of us all. Sometimes, our parents remember the strange things their children did at the age of two or twelve, and we often wish they would forget, but they will repeat those stories until we can never forget them. So at the age of nine, I cleaned out the pickle jar and at age ten, I was climbing the lampposts in the street like a circus artiste! I personally considered this a big achievement, but I did hide this ability of mine from my purely music-minded family. Whenever anybody would ask me to demonstrate, I would promptly and happily climb up the lamppost and even show off by reaching the top and waving with one hand. The thought that I could fall and break my bones, or something worse, never entered my mind. The friends I had in those days, mostly about the same age as I, were not up to such adventure. Perhaps this was the reason that some of them decided to tell on me. One day, they went behind my back to complain to my father so that I would be stopped from practising my lamppost trick.

That evening, when I reached home, my father casually told me that he had heard that I was an expert at climbing lampposts. Now I, innocent as I was, completely taken in by the casualness of his tone, thought that my father was showing his approval of my daring. So I promptly said yes. I was an expert. I could do what none of the other boys did. I dared. So then, my father asked me to show him how I did it. Pleased and proud, I went out with him and happily climbed the nearest lamppost. Would you believe that when I was midway, I even stopped and waved at my father? My father responded by asking me to show him if I could climb higher and suspecting nothing, I climbed to the top of the post. Much like a mountaineer scaling a peak, I felt thrilled with my conquest. There is a saying that the thrill does not last. I learnt this the hard way. For when I finally climbed down, I got what was waiting for me, and it was not a pat on the back! I got a sound beating, a long scolding, a lecture on broken bones and a warning to never repeat this feat. I never did.

My youngest child, Rabia, reminded me that I recently climbed up a tree to get some guavas for Sameer, my grandson. Ah, but a tree is not a lamppost, now, is it? Moreover, 2008, I tell her, is not recent! 'You were seventy-seven, Papa!' she says, in her best scolding voice. I laugh and ask her, 'Why, do you think I have become old?' Her reply is swift, 'Never, Papa! Climbing trees at seventy-seven! Who does that?' When did my children grow up so much? Well, perhaps climbing the lamppost was training of a different kind—for the things I would need to do for my grandchildren!

Both my father and my mother made sure I kept my commitment to my music practice and schedule, so that I developed the ability to focus, despite the distractions that all children experience. My dear mother, my Ammi, played a key part in my music, even as I trained under my father. When he could not be present to oversee my riyaz, he would delegate the responsibility to my mother. She would take this very seriously. My mother, with her background and understanding of music, knew both—the importance of riyaz and the correct way to do it. She would make me practice with dedication. She had many strategies that she would use with me, sometimes tempting me with goodies and sometimes scolding me. On rare occasions, I think I recall that she may have cuffed me once or twice for not focusing! She used to make sure that I was doing riyaz properly, and if I did not, she would report me to my father—then I really was in trouble.

I remember that I had a piggy bank she had made for me. It was just a hollow in the wall, and into this, she used to put away coins that she took from my father's money. These were savings. They were always useful. This was how I learnt the importance of stashing away a little money for when you may need it, or for when someone else may need it, and then you must help him or her. Whenever I needed some money, she would ask me to take it out from there, but she was so trusting and innocent that she never suspected me when sometimes, I took a little more than I had asked her for. I would laugh about it, but also felt guilty about betraying her trust. Strange as it may seem to you, these little habits I learnt growing up have stayed with me, even now that I am in the eighth decade of my life! I cannot imagine not having some savings of my own at hand, at home.

I continued to practise my music, do my riyaz and learn under the guidance of my uncle and guru, Ustad Fida Hussain Khan, who also lived in Badaun. In those days, learning music from a guru did not mean going to music class for an hour. It meant spending time with your guru, learning the intricacies of music from him, doing riyaz with him and also making yourself useful through service. This relationship is a little bit like being a member of the household. Teaching and learning were about more than a defined session of practice—they were integral to life. Each moment that you had the chance to observe, to share an experience, to learn a piece of wisdom, or as the teacher, to share a piece of wisdom, you did so.

Though the guru did not impose it, it was generally expected that if you were staying, eating and spending so much time in the guru's house, you would also take on the responsibilities of the household. There were many things to do. Fill water, attend to the plants, fetch something from the market if required, or do any odd jobs that had to be done. I was a very dedicated disciple and quite enjoyed sharing the responsibilities of my guru's household. I even used to clean and oil his bicycle regularly.

I was consumed by my desire to learn and to do riyaz. This was all I wanted to do, each waking moment. I remember being so consumed by music at about the age of twelve or thirteen that there was space for no other thought or desire, feeling or motivation. The frustration of time spent not doing riyaz was terrible. Distractions were irritating and unbearable. The ordinary routines of life that others held dear meant nothing to me. Thus, it was for days on end, afternoon succeeding afternoon, that I would find myself singing in the graveyard!

How I chanced upon this location, or the first time that I went there, I cannot recall, but I know I have spent many hours among the dead, with neither a sense of fear nor a sense of hesitation, wrapped up in my riyaz. These afternoons were spent so because my ustad would take his daily post-lunch siesta at that time. I was asked to go to my own house so that he would not be disturbed. In my own house too, I knew I would not find a space free of distraction. So I would run off to the local graveyard, which was desolate and quiet, a perfect place for me to do my riyaz. I did not have to worry about anybody listening to me, noting the mistakes I made, the false starts, the difficult parts that I would repeat, or even sometimes ignore. I could sing without any inhibition.

Today I look back at this period in my life and I see a child sitting inside a dilapidated tomb for hours, pleased with the shade and the relief from the harsh sun, playing a makeshift *tanpura* quickly put together by a local carpenter simply employing a metal wire and a piece of bamboo. The carpenter was a friend and he made this instrument for me for no charge. Another gift, another blessing I will always remember.

I was once this child. Perhaps this child still lives somewhere in me. The musical instruments used to be at my ustad sahib's house and I could not have brought a tanpura from there to do my own riyaz at the graveyard without informing someone. A tanpura would have cost twenty to forty rupees in those days, nothing by today's standards. At the time, however, it was a large sum and an amount that I could not afford. So after I finished my riyaz at the tomb, I would hide my precious tanpura behind some bushes and pray that it would stay safe till the next day. I did not want my family or my ustad to know that I was practising like this at the graveyard. Actually, I do not think I thought about it very much. I just did it, and it was my secret. I remember carrying my lunch from home and that was one chapatti. This I would split into two, keeping one half for my lunch break and reserving the second half for my post lunch hunger pangs at the tomb in the graveyard.

The funny part about the entire thing was that my ustad sahib thought that I had gone home to sleep in the afternoon and my family thought that I was at my ustad sahib's place. I was too young then to be sensitive to the fact that I was singing among the dead and departed. I was happy that there was no distraction, happy to be alone, but the realization that it was quiet there because the dead do not make any noise did not hit home. Not then. That child I remember lived an inner life of such intense focus that none of this was important. Such was my obsession for learning music and doing riyaz.

It was only many, many years later, when I revisited the place with my son, Rabbani, that I realized the meaning of disturbing the dead. For the first time, I felt a shiver go up my spine. Children can be so wrapped up in their world—or at least I was—that it matters little what is happening around them, or where they are. This could be one of the reasons that children learn so well, while adults often fight the urge to do and see multiple things together at the same time.

Still, did I ever think that my choice of place to practise music was strange? I look at that younger me and I wonder.

Papa talks about his childhood and his music education (taaleem) in a very matter-of-fact way, but I know that for a child to be trained at the feet of such illustrious masters of music such as Ustad Waris Hussain Khan, Ustad Fida Hussain Khan and Ustad Nissar Hussain Khan sahib is a matter of enormous pride. To perform at a concert before a large public audience at the age of eight is a great achievement. Papa speaks about his life and all that he has done very simply. This is a key aspect of his personality—his humility.

I think I should explain a few terms here for those who may be unfamiliar with them. Papa has spoken of gharanas and of the Senia tradition. The word 'Senia' is associated with mian Tansen, referring to music that owes its existence to him. Tansen is considered by many to be the father, or the founder, of Indian classical music. The word 'gharana' implies a style of music. The followers of Tansen's school of music are widely known as the followers of the 'Senia gharana' (i.e., 'Senia' style or school of music). The followers of this gharana could either be related to the family of Tansen, or have learnt and practised the style by virtue of being students in the tradition of the guru–shishya (teacher-disciple) method of keeping the knowledge of a tradition alive, or passing such knowledge on.

I think today about his first performance in Badaun on Janmashtami, which is celebrated by Hindus as Lord Krishna's birthday. This is a prime example of the Ganga-Jamuni tehzeeb or the fusion of Hindu and Muslim elements in the culture of north India. First of all, to have a Muslim chairperson of the local municipality organize an annual function on the occasion of Janmashtami, and then to have a little Muslim boy give his debut musical performance at the Hindu festival, these things sing of the spirit of a generation that must be respected and remembered. This is what India's history reflects, across art, culture, cuisine and social life.

We cherish this India.

It has been a little over five years that Rabbani and I have been married and I can tell you that my new life in this Muslim household has been simply one of bliss. Any fear, confusion or apprehensions that I may have had about adjusting in a Muslim household, with a different lifestyle, culture and outlook, were dispelled within the first few days of my marriage to Rabbani. I also realized that my fears about not being able to adjust in a family that followed a different religion were also unfounded.

My mother-in-law, whom I call Ammi, my dear father-in-law, whom I call Papa, my three brothers-in-law and their wives, my four sisters-in-law and their husbands, and all the children in the family treat me like their own. My religion is never discussed and I am never ever made to feel that I am not one of them.

My views are respected and all festivals are celebrated with equal fervour. The Mustafa Khan family is famous for having such aspects of a secular India. They follow their religion and respect all other religions and cultures too.

However, the one person who holds this large family together with love and care is my dear father-in-law, Ustad Ghulam Mustafa Khan. The soft-spoken, almost self-effacing, kind-hearted and gentle man that he is, he has always treated me like his own daughter.

In the chapter ahead, he has spoken of his childhood, when, as a young boy, he took decisions that caused his elders, family and gurus some anxiety. This was the 1940s, a time when he tumbled through troubled teenage years, even as the country raced towards Independence. As the decade ended, it wrought such events in his life that they remain with him even today. The child, too soon, would find himself taking on the responsibilities of a man, towards his family and towards himself.

The Rebel in Me

When I was fourteen years old, perhaps I did not care or did not know that riyaz, though integral to the practice and performance of music, must share some place and time with other elements of life, such as relationships and responsibility. This is always a difficult stage of life to be in, the child who is still growing up, wanting too soon to be independent and grown up. Now that I have children and grandchildren of my own, I understand that life has its stages and its phases, much like learning music, or for that matter, learning anything at all. Life is a learning curve, and for many, a constant yearning—for something else, for something more, for the next desire to be fulfilled, the next challenge of perfection and performance. This will always be there; this will outlast you and me. When we are very young, we are not always aware of this. You cannot know what you do not know. It is as simple as that.

After some time, I began to feel that all these 'other' activities, chores and household duties at my ustad sahib's place were taking up too much of my time and diverting my focus from my true purpose, which was learning Hindustani classical music from my guru. Therefore, I started avoiding doing the chores that I had been performing on a regular basis for many months. The family members of my guru noticed this. Since they had become used to my taking care of some chores every day, my sudden change disrupted their schedules and, naturally, upset them. Nobody said anything directly to me, but I could sense their displeasure, and that was an even bigger distraction than the chores I was no longer doing.

It is a measure of my immaturity then that I grew so upset at this, that all I could think of was how to free myself from what seemed like a big hurdle to learning! My sole ambition was to learn, practice, learn and practice, and to continue to do only that and nothing else. I knew that if I complained to my parents, they would tell me that there was nothing wrong in helping out with the household chores, so I decided that speaking to them would be futile. I pondered over the options that I had and felt that I did not really have any. Not in Badaun. So I decided to run away.

I left Badaun and travelled by bus to a small town called Atwa, in district Sitapur. I think that I was both blessed and lucky because while aimlessly roaming around this unknown, unfamiliar town, I met Thakur Ismail. He used to be a disciple of my grandfather and was now the zamindar of seventy-five villages. He recognized me and asked me what I was doing alone and so far away from home. I had no choice but to tell him the truth. If I step away from this recollection and look at it with the wisdom of the years that have passed between then and now, I see how difficult it must have been for him to listen to me and take responsibility for me, for that is exactly what he did. I hesitantly told him my story and how I was not getting enough time to do my riyaz in

Badaun. I was scared that he would report this to my father and my guru and send me back. He did neither of those things. He heard me out patiently and then offered me his home as a place to stay and practice. I was overjoyed with the sudden option that had appeared before me, but then he said that he would need to inform my parents that I was with him. I stopped him mid-sentence, because I knew that if my parents heard of this, they would immediately come and take me back home. This was in the mid-1940s. The telephone was a rarity. You did not just carry one in your pocket. Not every home had one, nor did every shop or even every street corner. I think there were whole cities and towns that existed without telephone lines in those days. So my parents were not a phone call away. You had the post and telegraph service. Enough time for a runaway to run away again! I put on my most determined face and told Thakur Ismail, '*Aap agar aisa karenge toh main yahan se bhi bhaag jaaoonga* (If you inform them, I will run away from here as well)!'

Thakur Ismail was a wise man, apart from being a great lover of music himself. He used to play the harmonium with one hand while he prepared the accounts of the farmer's dues with the other! I have seen him do this. Anyway, the result of my obstinacy and threats to run away again was that he promised me that he would not inform my family and that I was welcome to do my riyaz at his house.

I certainly believed all was well and my plan was working out. I settled in as a part of the Thakur household and happily passed my days and nights as I desired, doing my riyaz. However, if I had thought that all was going to be exactly as I wanted, I was wrong. I, the child who practised on a makeshift tanpura among the graves in a tomb of the local graveyard in Badaun, got the fright of my life one night. I was deeply engrossed in my riyaz when suddenly, I felt something, or rather I felt that I was being watched by someone. I turned my head to see a figure with a black face, covered in a big blanket, staring at me. It was silent and unmoving. I froze. I was terrified. Suddenly this figure seemed to flash fire and ash from its mouth. My knees shook, and though I wanted to call out for help, I could not speak. It left without doing anything to me, but I could no longer continue my riyaz.

The next day I developed a high fever because of the scary encounter. Thakur Ismail was deeply concerned and I told him that I had seen a ghost. It did not take him much time to figure out what was going on. He was not a believer in ghosts. Soon enough, he had caught the culprit. It was the next door neighbour, who said he was disturbed by my late night riyaz and just wanted to scare me. At that, of course, he had succeeded. Ah, how many pains he took in his effort! He had painted his face with kajal (kohl), filled ash in his mouth and lit two matchsticks between his teeth to add to the drama. Thakur Ismail, in his anger at the man, put a gun to his head to warn him of dire consequences if he ever tried something like that again. Then he told me, in front of him, that I should practise without any fear and whenever I wished. Perhaps this was not fair, but in those days, all I really wanted was to be left alone. I practiced for nearly sixteen hours a day, every day. I stayed with the Thakurs for almost four months.

Then one day, I received a telegram from Radio Lucknow. They invited me to perform live at the radio station! Was this not my dream? I was perhaps just fourteen or fifteen when I sang on the radio for everyone to hear. Well, apart from whoever else did or did not hear me, my father certainly heard me singing on the radio. He promptly reached Lucknow and the next thing I knew, I was back in Badaun. I think it is well that I have no recollection of the things he said to me when he came to get me. I remember there were long periods of silence as we travelled home. My father was a strict man, but affectionate too. I think running away from home was possibly one of the worst things I had ever done. It caused him enormous worry, it caused everyone great anxiety at home. I do remember thinking that I would not know how to face my mother when we reached. I think I am grateful to the years that have passed for the fact that I remember nothing of that homecoming.

From then on, I diligently learnt music at the feet of Ustad Fida Hussain Khan and his son, Ustad Nissar Hussain Khan, my third guru.

The 1940s were a turbulent time in world history. The little adventures and misadventures of the child that I was, would have held no meaning or significance for anyone except my family and my gurus. I think back to those days and I know that I really did not think too much about the world outside the sheltered space of my hometown and my music. Yet, I recall that it was 1945 when I was brought back home by my father from Lucknow. India was just two years away from achieving Independence. I was in Badaun in 1947 during the Independence Day celebrations, a part of the celebration of freedom that took place all over the country. Children can be as innocent as you allow them to be and more. I know that I was one such innocent child. I have an intense memory of singing patriotic songs, '*deshgana*', with my whole heart and soul, one among the many children and youngsters of India, who sang with deep joy and pride. Strangely, I also recall that each child received a laddoo in celebration, and that I, because I had the formal status of a singer among the students, received two! Memory is a strange thing. We recall moments and experiences that may seem irrelevant and unimportant when seen in the larger context, but this is the material that often defines the life of a person.

Then there are other personal milestones that change you in significant ways. Inevitably, loss is one of them; a part of life, inescapable. In 1948, Ustad Fida Hussain Khan sahib passed away. He was just seventy-five. I was seventeen years old.

I remember very well that he lay on his deathbed with his head on my lap. He could barely recognize anybody, and his breath was laboured, difficult. He was unconscious of the saliva that trickled from the side of his mouth and I wiped it away with care. He looked up at me as I did this. My father was there too. Thinking that ustad sahib was trying to remember who I was, he told him, '*Bhai, yeh aapka* Ghulam *hai*' (*Brother, he is your Ghulam*—for those who do not know, the word 'ghulam' also means slave).' I will always remember my guru's reply. As I remember this, I feel tears in my eyes and my heart constricts. He said, '*Yeh mera ghulam nahin, yeh mera gulaab hai* (*He is not my slave, he is my rose*).'

His passing hit me as nothing else before had done. I was devastated. Without consciously thinking so, or ever stating so, I considered him my father, my guru and my guide. Now he was gone. It took me a long time to come to terms with this grief. Relationships do not pass away because people pass away. They remain in your heart and soul; they become a part of you. You will always miss the people who are gone. That loss never really goes away. So much of all that I am, is because of Ustad Fida Hussain Khan sahib. May his great soul rest in peace.

For a long while, music and practice became my refuge. I dedicated my efforts to my gurus. Now I trained entirely under Ustad Nissar Hussain Khan sahib. It became a critical part of my routine, for I felt that with the passing of my guru, my childhood had passed too. If before this, I was passionate about riyaz, then the intensity of that passion increased even further. As a result, I think that my focus and expertise at what I was learning improved greatly. The very next year, in 1949, at the age of eighteen, I became an All India Radio-approved and graded artiste. I started performing for the radio.

At that time, AIR had only six stations—Delhi, Madras, Calcutta, Bombay, Lucknow and Tiruchirappalli. Lucknow was considered a big centre. I was fortunate to have been approved from Lucknow. I was actually allowed to perform live. I do not know how many people were able to listen to the radio then, or how many people had radios. I felt very proud to be a part of this new generation of inventions. My salary was Rs 80 per performance. In today's terms it is nothing, but in those days, it was considered a sizeable amount.

I migrated to Lucknow with the blessings of my guru, my father, my ammi, and with the love and support of my family. Lucknow was a bigger city. I had even more love and affection for the city as it was the city of Nawab Wajid Ali Shah, where my ancestors had been court musicians. The history of this city was tied up with the history of my family, and I was happy to explore what the city had in store for me.

This time, I was not a runaway. I needed a place to stay in this unfamiliar city. I was introduced to a kind woman who agreed to provide me space to live and do my riyaz. My independence was of great value to me, but it brought me to a place where I had to learn to contend on my own with a world that was not always happy to hear me sing. One of my neighbours, a judge, would get disturbed by my singing. One day, he threatened me and said that if I did not stop doing my riyaz at odd hours, he would call the police and have me arrested. This time there was no Thakur Ismail to help me, nor could I call my father from Badaun to take me home. My landlady, not wanting to annoy the judge, asked me to stop doing my riyaz there.

I was disappointed at this, but was determined to find a way. I discovered another room, which was lying unused, under the staircase at the rear of the house. It was filthy. That did not deter me. I grabbed a bucket of water, brooms and some cloth, and spent a day airing and cleaning out that room. This was a good place to practice. To eliminate the chances of anyone getting disturbed by my singing, I devised a method to muffle the sound. It was a simple method. I would do my riyaz with my head inside a *matka* (a matka is an earthen pot generally used to store water)! My system worked, and I like to think that the matka became somewhat proficient in music too. I adjusted to this routine over time without too much difficulty. Or perhaps I chose to ignore the difficulty. My method worked, my neighbours were no longer trying to throw me out of the neighbourhood and my riyaz remained a part of my nightly routine.

These new attempts at living and learning on my own were soon disrupted. My mother was unwell and I returned home.

My dearest Ammi.

I remember this period so well. I came home to find her terribly ill and in bed. She had tuberculosis, or TB, as it was called. TB was a big problem and it was frightening. I think my mother may not have known she was unwell till her ill health became too much for her to bear. She was not one to complain much. I was so used to her doing the things she did at home and with us, that I never gave her presence a second thought. She was even integral to my learning music. To see her now, mostly in bed, too weak to get up or do anything, scared me. I felt helpless.

One day, I wanted to get her something. I dipped my hand into the old hollow wall piggy and found it empty. My hand swept the sides and bottom. Nothing. Not even a small coin. Surprised, I turned towards her. She looked at me silently, and then the tears welled up in her eyes. I think they welled up in mine too. Neither of us needed to say anything to the other. I ran to her, stumbling, shocked, and held her hand. I had no idea, wrapped up as I was in my one passion, that this was the state of things at home. She told me that all the money in the piggy had gone towards her treatment and medicines. Then she burst out weeping. I can still hear the sound of her crying. It wrenches my soul.

She never recovered from her illness and died a few days later.

Too much loss came too swiftly and too soon, and my childhood slipped away. I was nineteen when these events happened. Even after so many years, at eighty-seven years old, whenever I remember my ammi's last days, my eyes brim with tears.

Since I was the eldest among my siblings, I had more responsibilities now. The unfortunate events of the recent past meant that our family fortunes had received a blow. Money had earlier not been a problem; we were a well-to-do family. Most of the money went into treating the terrible illness that took the precious lives of three of my family—my mother and my sisters.

As the oldest brother, I was almost equal to a father. I had to make my younger siblings feel that whatever may happen, I was going to be there and would always stand by them. I cannot even imagine not being there or not doing something for my family. As far as I was able to do anything, and if it was my responsibility to do something for any or all of them, I would do it. There was no compulsion; I would willingly do anything for them. This was true then and this is true now. We are supported by our families, we are held together through difficulties and griefs, hard times and lows, by our families. They share our joys and achievements, they are happy with us and for us. We have to be there for them in the same way. This is how a strong family is made. At least, this is what I have learnt in my life and I hope I have been able to pass it on to my children.

Papa has always been deeply committed to his family. The passing away of his ammi and his two sisters caused him great anguish. He loved his siblings and even in the re-telling of those events, which happened decades ago, I have seen his mood become cloudy because there is a grief that remains with him even today.

The celebrated Ustad Rashid Khan is Papa's nephew and the son of one of his sisters, Shakri Begum, who passed away in 1973. He is a well-known singer, an exponent of the Rampur-Sahaswan gharana, and a 2006 Padma Shri awardee. For a short while, when he was very young, Papa taught him music.

From all that I have personally experienced of my marital home and family, I know that the bonds between parents and children, older and younger siblings, the new entrants into the family such as me and the other family members, are of utmost importance to Papa.

In the way he reflects on and speaks of his childhood and youth, even the early decade of his marriage to Ammi, I think Papa has lived with a feeling of not being able to be in two places, doing different things, at the same time. What I mean is, his focus on his music and riyaz was so strong that he seems to have lived with a feeling that there was something more he could do for his family. Sometimes, I am almost sure that he has been making up for those times in his childhood when music, only music, was his priority, by doing his best to give of himself—his time, energy and care—to his children and then his grandchildren.

The gentle person I have come to know so well has had to deal with people and events that have not been either gentle or easy. If someone else were to have told me that Papa once spent many occasions at his house playing music for someone I can only describe today as a ruffian, who once actually threatened him, I would never believe it.

Ustad Ghulam Mustafa Khan has encountered all kinds of people, not all of them music aficionados, and some of them took rivalry and insecurity to the level of the absurd.

Papa's stories of his life in the '50s are fascinating and sometimes hard to believe!

The Fifties—Early Years of
My Independence

Until my younger siblings grew a little older and became more capable of taking care of themselves, I felt uncomfortable about leaving Badaun. At the same time, it was becoming increasingly apparent that to make something of myself and the years of effort put into my training by my parents and gurus, I had to relocate to another town or city centre, where there were supportive patrons and audiences passionate about art and music.

Post-Independence, the country was moving forward swiftly in more ways than I can describe here. It was an exciting time of great changes everywhere. The state in which lay my home town of Badaun was called United Provinces by the British. That was how I had known it in my childhood. Now, in the '50s, it was renamed Uttar Pradesh. Many towns and cities of historical and modern importance seemed to offer rich opportunities for an artiste. The immensely important institution, the Sangeet Natak Akademi of India, was set up in the early '50s. That this academy was to play a crucial role in the promotion, protection, support and development of our country's artistic and cultural heritage was indicated from the very beginning. If you look up their historical archives today, you will find recordings of the greats from that era and generation, names familiar to us all, both then and now, whom we speak of with respect, pride and joy— Ustad Mushtaq Hussain Khan, Ustad Nissar Hussain Khan, Pandit Bhimsen Joshi, Pandit Ram Narain, Pandit Radhika Mohan Moitra, Ustad Shaik Dawood Khan sahib, Ustad Amir Khan sahib, Pandit Ravi Shankar, Ustad Bade Ghulam Ali Khan sahib.

There are so many from that powerful time in history. A time that I was lucky to have been a part of, to have witnessed, to have experienced in my own way. Radio became an increasingly familiar part of life in the '50s. The first of the national music programmes began to be broadcast in the early part of the decade. The first Radio Sangeet Sammelan was held in 1954. You will know it as Akashvani Sangeet Sammelan. Yes, it continues even today, an annual event organised by AIR in different places across India. It began in my time, when I was a young man. It was a wonderful way to promote our musical heritage, to make classical music popular, to let us, musicians from different gharanas, get a chance to hear the music and the styles of each other's traditions. The world was opening up for those who sought to explore it. I certainly did, through my music. I started performing for these Sangeet Sammelans from the very beginning, when the programme started. I continued to perform for them over the years. I enjoyed them very much. Over the years, radio became a wonderful way to connect with the ordinary person whom you may not otherwise meet, who may not come for a live classical music concert.

What is a radio today? Every car has one. There was a time that almost every home had one. Radio reached the villages in India. It is a wonderful piece of technology.

From Badaun, among the cities I could have gone to, there was Lucknow, where I had learnt to do my riyaz with my head in a matka. I realize that is not a formal introduction to the city, but it is certainly a personal memory that moves me to wonder whether it was really me that lived that life. It is easier looking back at those memories now, and I am happy I am not there today. At the same time, I do know that the person that I am now, is born of the person that I was, so I accept my experiences, and am grateful to them as well. Another city with possibilities accessible to me was Kanpur. Kanpur was nearby and if I were to move there, home would not seem too far away, I thought. I discussed this possibility with my family and they encouraged me to set out and try things again. I have a feeling that the loss of my ammi was harder to bear living in the home where her presence was everywhere. Now her absence and the silence that took the place of her voice made it hard to focus on music, on listening, on learning or on practice.

That is how I found myself in Kanpur. I had a place to stay and I was settling in. To others, settling in may mean putting your clothes into a cupboard, making sure the kitchen has tea and sugar and opening the windows to see the view outside, smiling uncertainly at your new neighbours, exchanging names and introductions, perhaps.

Settling in, to me, has always meant riyaz. Unfortunately, my riyaz unsettled my neighbours again. I now found myself at the receiving end of the noisy wrath of those who lived near me. I would ignore them when I could, be quiet and unobtrusive when I had to leave or enter my house, and give explanations about the importance of practice to a singer when I had the opportunity. The complaining and yelling did not stop, though, and some days, my spirits sank so low that I contemplated giving up and going home again.

Things reached such a point that one of the neighbours hired some *goondas* (roughnecks) and instructed them to harass me until I stopped or left the neighbourhood. I have not always had a fan following, as you can see! One day, I was walking down the road, engrossed in riyaz, keeping my voice low. It is possible that anyone who noticed would think that I was not all there. Is that how you say it? I did not care. Suddenly, someone pushed so hard against me that I stumbled and almost fell. My immediate reaction was of shock and anger. However, I was not sure if it was an accident, and I turned around to look at the person who had walked into me. He was a burly, rough-looking person who stared down at me with no hint of an apology. In fact, the fellow did not move back even a step and menacingly growled at me, 'Are you blind? Can't you see where you're going?' To me it sounded clearly as if he was looking for a fight. I almost put my hand up, an instinctive reaction to defend myself against the threat of attack. Some other wisdom or presence of mind guided me. I was not afraid, and I was determined to change this situation through my behaviour. I stood my ground, I did not step back, I folded my hands and apologized to him even though I knew it was not my fault. I told him politely, 'Forgive me, brother. I was lost in my own thoughts and did not bump into you intentionally.'

Have you ever experienced an interaction with someone who is a stranger, but you can almost witness the thought process taking place in his or her head? He looked at me, his frown deepened, but at the same time, his eyes grew puzzled. I could almost see a change of plan and a struggle happen within him. He stepped back and without a word, turned around and walked away. I stood there and suddenly realized that I was shaking, a physical reaction to a situation that was alien to me.

Fighting and aggression are not in my nature. I do not practise these things; I do not consider them pride-worthy. I have met different kinds of people in my life. No matter who the person is and what the situation, I have always believed that it is your intent, expressed or silent, that communicates what you need to. My intent never was and never has been to harm another, or to hurt the body, mind, feelings or soul of another. My intent is not to put myself in harm's way either. These two things close the door to violence and aggression in my life.

Is it important in the autobiography of an artiste to share these things? To me it is important that as a medium, a channel for the music or art that expresses itself through me, I remain clean in thought, intention and action. Perhaps I would not have been able to state this as clearly those many years ago, but I know today that I have always lived this way. As an artiste, this is part of my respect for God and my respect for the art form to which I have devoted my life, which has given me so many gifts through the years.

Coming back to my encounter with the man who bumped into me, I found out later that this man went back to the neighbour who had sent him to hit me and abused him. I heard that he said that I was a decent human being, not someone who deserved to be harmed or threatened. I found this out from the man himself, and from some of his strange friends. I call them his friends, not a gang of roughnecks, because among them there was a strong sense of friendship as well as of right and wrong. One day, soon after the incident on the street, I found him at my door again. I was more than a bit taken aback, and a little disturbed that he should come back thus. He looked at me unsmiling, but what he said was also, in its own way, part of the poetry and music of life.

He apologized for his behaviour. He went on to say that I should rest easy; nobody in this neighbourhood was going to harm me. He turned to leave, but I stopped him and invited him in for chai. If someone is at your door, you do not turn them away or let them leave without an expression of respect, welcome and friendship. This is what I said to him. He smiled at this, and hesitantly, he came in. This was the start of a strange new friendship. He became a fan of my music and soon he brought his friends to visit me and hear me sing. Today, I think about it and realize that these were strange gatherings for me, but I also know that music is my blessing. Music connects us all across vast differences of culture, personality and ways of being.

Soon I realized that I was becoming increasingly well-known and popular. Where once the neighbours looked at me as if they wished me gone, they now began to visit me and request me to sing for them. There were some performances, some stage shows, at which I am happy to say, I was becoming a bit of a hit! Had popularity been my life's goal, I certainly began to achieve it then. It was not my goal, but it was a happy by-product of my becoming increasingly better, not just because of the practice that was a part of my routine, but practice at performing before audiences of different kinds.

Very few people today have heard of a programme called Sangeet Dhara. It was quite popular then, and it was a big thing to be a performer at Sangeet Dhara. It tested a musician's expertise and I think it required one to have the stamina and ability of a marathon runner. Continuous music was performed for twelve hours in a sort of relay fashion. Therefore, it was a non-stop session of music where if a tanpura player got tired, he would signal another tanpura player to take over, and likewise for tabla players, sarangi players and others. The vocalists who got tired of singing non-stop would also gesture to another singer to keep the session of non-stop music going.

I participated in a Sangeet Dhara session and I hold the distinction of singing non-stop for ten hours there. I am very sure that I would have made it through the entire twelve hours, but my concentration was broken by one of the organizers. He offered me a glass of milk to drink!

Now I shall tell you something you must never forget. There is a kind of an experience of art that sometimes a singer, a composer, a writer might have (perhaps even a scientist or mathematician will recognize this), an experience where you transcend time, place and situation. Momentarily, you transcend the limitations of your tiny human self. For me, this experience has been devotional. I have heard the young people of today who work in films and recording studios refer to this experience somewhat casually as the 'zone'. Is that right? Zone. No matter what they call it, many of them do understand it. A glass of milk, a sip of water, a towel to wipe the sweat off the brow—these, to one who is observing such a person, may seem, from the kindness and concern of your heart, to be the need of the hour. Unless you know the artiste well, unless you know what they need when they are in the middle of an experience such as this, do not risk distracting them with anything at all. They will not thank you. That glass of milk and the look of anxiety on the face of the poor fellow who offered it to me, broke my concentration. They cut through that experience that I was in the middle of, that I had given myself up to, and I had to stop. I signalled to another singer who took up the performance where I left it. I had not the breath left in me to refuse the one who still held in his hand that glass of milk, nor did I have the heart to rebuke him. He just did not know any better.

However, that performance of mine at Sangeet Dhara was a milestone in my life as a singer and musician. People heard of my marathon session. I was becoming a familiar name, and it seems that other young artistes, singers and musicians were being inspired by me. Soon, this took me to the next point of learning in my life. I was requested to teach! I, who all these years had seen myself as a student, a practitioner of traditions of music passed on to me by my gurus. It may surprise you to know that the two roles continue to co-exist peacefully side-by-side in my life. As I slowly took on the role of teacher, I did not relinquish the discipline and systems of a student. The day you stop learning or feel that you know all there is to know, is the day you are done for. I am not yet done for! I am a teacher, but I will stay a student forever.

I must also acknowledge with gratitude the many gifts life has showered upon me, that I felt blessed that my commitment to music was opening the doors to sustenance and support for myself and for those of my family who needed me. An important part of independence is being able to sustain yourself and support your family, or at least contribute to supporting them. Sometimes we confuse independence with the capacity to earn a living, but I see them as two different things. They are linked, but separate.

Life was changing swiftly. My popularity was growing. I will always be grateful to my father for the early self-discipline and self-awareness he sought to nurture in me along with the music. It took one neighbour to compliment me as a child, for my father to become alert to my reactions and responses to it. If he cuffed me over the head and increased my practice schedule all those years ago, it was only because he did not want me, as a child, to develop too great a sense of my importance or begin to take things easy. Later it came naturally to me to build compartments between what my audiences thought of me and my knowledge of myself and of my art. Self-assessment and riyaz never lost their significance and importance in my life. Do not misunderstand me here. The love and appreciation from my audience matters to me. At the same time, I feel that it is the music that they love; it is the music that causes them to show me affection and faith. I therefore must continue to hone my skills, to be true to them and to the music that connects us, the audience and me.

As fame increased and popularity grew, there was some fallout too. There were people in the circle of musical arts who had a very different view of themselves and of art and artistes. To them, another artiste did not become a friend and companion in a space to be shared and explored together. Another artiste was a rival. This was something for which I was not prepared. I was unprepared for the jealousy and active efforts to humiliate or sabotage another human being. One of the first few occasions in my life that I recall experiencing the disgruntlement of people like this was when Ram Babu Telang organized a show at Merchant Chambers, Civil Lines, Kanpur. I had settled into the performance and so had the audience. All was going well when it rained on me. There was a sudden shower of water, poured upon me by someone who was backstage, who was never caught. This water damaged my tanpura and I could not use it any longer for this performance. I gently set it aside as I continued to sing. I cannot say I was undisturbed—I was. In fact, for just a moment, I felt panic set in. Perhaps it was the shock of the water, the realization that someone actually did this to me, and then seeing my tanpura damaged.

What am I without my tanpura? More than an act of sabotage, this is violence against the soul and spirit of a performer. This happened in front of everyone, and the audience witnessed it. The support that I felt from them was overwhelming, for they saw what had happened and they understood that I was continuing my performance despite the shock. Artistes and performers often say that they feel a connection with the audience and that always works wonders. I can truly say that this performance and connect with the audience saw me through what could have been a disaster. This was not the only time I was harassed in Kanpur. A number of shows were organized in the city and I was invited to perform at most of them. Organizers would tell me their event was incomplete without my presence.

There grew another section of people, the ones who live their lives in the narrow confines of petty rivalry and competitiveness, who despised the attention being showered upon me by both the audience and students. It was overwhelming. It began to affect my mood and worse, it began to affect my focus and my riyaz. Negative thoughts and feelings can be as damaging as actions. Torn between both, I often wondered what to do. I did not want to leave my newly built wealth of fame and popularity, to start again elsewhere with new and unknown problems. I became fed up with the situation. This was precisely what the unhappy spiteful lot wanted to achieve, I think. Then something very important happened.

In 1957, the great musicologist and guru, Acharya K.C. Deva Brihaspati, who was doing some research and compiling the Indian Music Samvedh, asked me to be a part of the project. He had known me since I was just an infant and he was at the Rampur court. In Kanpur, he heard me perform for a radio concert, and immediately after the performance he got in touch with me. He wanted me to sing compositions derived from the Natyashastra and Brihat Deshi written by Matang Rishi, and from Dev's Sangeet Ratnakar based on Jati Gaan. I have been given to believe that I am the only artiste in 700 years who has revived the old tradition. The Sangeet Natak Akademi of India has preserved thirty minutes each from the seven records of my singing from those ancient granths.

At the time, there were some opinions that a Muslim artiste shouldn't work with Hindu granths. The determined Acharyaji did not let this deter him. Despite the strong protests and opposition, he asked me to carry on with my work.

There is something else that I remember about this time and this project. It may or may not seem relevant to many, but I did not eat meat, garlic or onions as a mark of respect for the people and the traditions represented by the compositions I was singing, for the entire duration that I worked on the project. I did not want to hurt anybody's sentiments. This was not very difficult for me to do, because I ate to live, I did not live to eat. It did not really matter to me, therefore, what I ate or did not eat. I simply thanked God for every meal, and continued to respect the traditions that surrounded the work I did and the people I worked with.

Somewhere, unspoken, in my heart, I felt that when we are given the opportunity to connect with the spirit and soul of a teacher and an ancient tradition, one must, for a time, dissolve and free the self to experience fully that other unfamiliar wisdom and way of being.

Bombay—My Karam Bhoomi

I was twenty-six years old when I worked on the Indian Music Samvedh for Acharya Brihaspati. Despite some hard times in Kanpur, I am grateful to God that I stayed on as I did. This persistence in the face of opposition may also have been due to a streak of obstinacy in my nature. I think it is wrong to hound another person, insult them, or attempt to bring them down. I will not step down or give in to unfairness. I have sustained my focus and kept to my work. I appreciate the art and effort of another artiste, and I respect the feelings of another human being. I continue to do my best by my music. That has occupied my life!

After completing the project with Acharyaji, I was free to decide what course I should choose next. It was a project of great note and esteem and again, I received a great deal of attention for having worked on it. So I found myself with an invitation to come to Bombay—much farther afield than I had ever been before. My life was changing and I was ready to embrace these changes. In Bombay, there lived a music lover by the name of Babubhai Banker. He used to organize extravagant and beautiful *mehfils* (gatherings) at his home with legendary musicians of that time. Babubhai had heard me at a concert earlier and began to take an interest in my career as a musician. He invited me one day to perform at a mehfil in his home. This, by itself, was a very big move forward in my work, but you cannot imagine how I felt when I arrived for my performance and realized something else. In the notice about the mehfil, where my name as performer was mentioned, he had added the word 'Ustad' to my name! Ustad? Me? At the age of twenty-six, I was certainly far from thinking of myself as one, though I admired and respected many. I think that perhaps I froze for a moment when I read that.

Not only was this the day that I became Ustad Ghulam Mustafa Khan, it was also the day that for the very first time, I performed live before other stalwarts of music. The other invitees included Ustad Bade Ghulam Ali Khan sahib, Ustad Amir Khan sahib, Anjanibai Malpekar and many others. While I was delighted to hear this, I was also nervous and afraid of singing in front of all these greats. Think of it. All of them older, much more experienced, more practised, wiser in music and life, than I. Ustad Bade Ghulam Ali Khan sahib, exponent of the Patiala gharana, was known for his own unique mixing of different styles of music. I think he had just moved to Bombay, but his reputation had spread long ago and far beyond any borders of city and state. Ustad Amir Khan sahib of Indore, known as the founder of the Indore gharana, had already cut music records at a time when I was perhaps not even five years old and did not know what a record was! Anjanibai Malpekar—who had by this time stopped singing, and was a teacher of music. The next year, she would receive a Sangeet Natak Akademi Fellowship, though of course I did not know this at the time.

All known names, each one a legend. I, at twenty-six, see the prefix 'ustad' attached to my name for the first time in my life, just before I am to perform before them. There are some moments and experiences in your life that you will always remember with the same freshness no matter how many years pass. For me, this mehfil at Babubhai Banker's is one such.

To regain control over my overwhelmed self and to calm my nerves, I went to the balcony of the house to do some last-minute riyaz. I had just about begun, and the familiar practice was bringing the comfort of security to me, when I had that feeling, that sensation that you are not alone. I spun around and saw a tall, bulky figure of a man with a great moustache standing behind me. Ustad Bade Ghulam Ali Khan sahib. I was startled and instantly recognized him. I bowed to him, as is the way of showing courtesy and respect, and I sought his blessings. Whatever little calming of my nerves that I had hoped to achieve . . . well, now everything had begun to hum and spin instead. My stomach was lurching. You see, it takes time to achieve a maturity in which, in the presence of greatness, you can remain anchored to a strong sense of self. I had not quite achieved that then!

'So you are the boy who is singing tonight?' he asked, with a face that gave away nothing. I could just barely nod, so I did, wondering what was to come. He observed me in all seriousness, and in his face now, I saw that he knew exactly what I was feeling. His voice was kind. 'I was wondering who this Ustad Ghulam Mustafa Khan is. Yes, I have heard that you sing very well,' he said. Before turning away, he gave me his blessings. Suddenly my churning stomach and buzzing nerves settled. I did not have to do anything. No riyaz, no deep breaths. I understood something. The presence that you bring to any space influences that space and the others in it. This presence is not something heard, nor necessarily seen. It is felt. That is how you can calm a person, or agitate them, threaten them or support them. These small lessons in life have come to me through my music and have become a part of who I am.

That day I sang Raag Bihaag for one-and-a-half hours in front of these experts. Ustad Bade Ghulam Ali Khan was known for his thumris. So on that day, I did dare to do something else. I sang a thumri in Raag Pilu with my own variations. I know that I enjoyed that performance and while I was singing, I did, as I always do, give myself to the music. When I finished singing, I looked at him first and I saw that he was smiling. Then he got up, came to me, put his hand over my head and said, 'God bless you, my son. You sing very well and fully deserve to be called an ustad.'

Words have their limitations. I cannot express to you what I felt when he said this to me. I only knew that then I was truly at a turning point in my life. Nowadays, everyone wants a certificate, a piece of paper with a name on it. I come from a different time. These relationships and these interactions, these were the certificates you received, not printed on paper; you could neither frame them nor store them in a dusty cupboard. These became a part of your soul.

I bowed my head in front of Ustad Bade Ghulam Ali Khan sahib and thanked him. I bowed before each of the others, for they too were generous with their compliments and their blessings. Thus, I became Ustad Ghulam Mustafa Khan.

Why is it that two or two hundred different individuals can sing the same composition, and yet, each person's singing is unique and sounds different? I am not even referring to the variations that an artiste may bring to their rendering of a piece. I think it is because of the people themselves. The person is in the song they are singing; you cannot separate the singer from that song, and this is true of every rendition. In the stories you read in this autobiography, there is so much about the person Ustad Ghulam Mustafa Khan. His particular philosophical approach to life makes his music what it is.

How did the rest of us manage to find our way into this story of a man and his music, of the single-minded passion and pursuit of song? After all, he was completely lost in his music and riyaz.

It is well within the realm of possibility that had it not been for the intervention of ustad sahib's father, marriage and family would have been just words and concepts in Papa's life, experienced only through his own childhood experiences of the relationship between his parents and his own relationships with his siblings. He spared no time to even think of matters such as his own marriage and starting a family.

The decade of the '60s brought about massive life changes, both in the realm of the personal, and in the realm of music, for ustad sahib. Before the best things happen, there are always a few hiccups. Perhaps these are the indicators that the best is on its way. In this case, I am speaking of the way in which ustad sahib and my ammi, my mother-in-law, Amina Begum, met and got married. It was not simple, but then when it happened, it was exactly as God meant it to be.

This decade of the '60s was to be the busiest that Papa had possibly ever experienced. Perhaps it was more challenging because the story of the man and his music was now a story of the family man and his music. Papa, with his inherent sense of connection to the concept and responsibilities of family, grew steadily into his role as husband. It took him time to prepare himself for the independence that he felt he needed to have before he and his wife could actually share a roof of their own and build a home together.

It seems to be perfectly in keeping with the nature of this man, that he went about his preparation to be a good husband and later a good father, with the same deep understanding and discipline, which he brought to bear on his passionate pursuit of music. The process of creating a musical composition requires the maestro to bring together different elements of music. Papa turned his life into a blend of elements, an ever-evolving composition, in which he regularly practised the weaving of his love and care for his family into a life that demanded focused attention to his art.

So these are the stories of change, of adjustments made by not just one man but by his family, those already a part of his life, and the others yet to be. Behind music and the evolution of an artiste stands life itself. Papa connects with a wide and diverse audience at a practical, an emotional and a spiritual level. For this to happen, there are layers of learning and living that a person must acquire. In the takeaway from these experiences, there is an invisible contribution to all that you present to the world.

My Wife, My Humsafar

One day, my father spoke to me about marriage.

Yes, it was as sudden as that.

After that tremendous day at Babubhai Banker's house, I visited Bombay often. I loved the city. There was a sense of joy in our home at Badaun. I would tell my stories and I would see the pride on my father's face, on the faces of all in the family. My riyaz routine continued as always, unaffected by the way a new world was beginning to open up to me. I was content.

Then came this talk about marriage.

It is always a little strange, this conversation, when it happens between parents and children. There is something about it that takes preparation of some sort—mental, emotional and spiritual. The subject of marriage is somehow a symbol of a great life change, no matter what you have achieved before or what you may achieve after. Everyone seems to consider marriage as one of those routine, expected aspects of life but when it comes down to it, and you deal with the thought, there is nothing routine about it!

For one thing, you may no longer think about yourself as just yourself, alone in the space you occupy in life. Now you must think of sharing space and of learning to share space with a person you may not know. My space was almost wholly taken over by music and riyaz. What would it be like to open this space out to the influence of another? Not just any other, but another who is to be my partner through life? A *humsafar* (fellow traveller)? I think these thoughts flashed through my head in an instant. I did not have the words for them. They may have been feelings. My father, having brought me up with discipline and affection, understood them. He told me to take things one step at a time, just as it is with learning music—you take one step at a time.

Soon, the whispered word was out in a small circle of family and close friends that the marriage of Ustad Waris Hussain Khan's son, Ustad (yes) Ghulam Mustafa Khan, was now under discussion.

I am married to Amina Begum, but before this marriage could happen, there was what you may call a lucky hit-and-miss! I might tell you this story in a light-hearted way, but be in no doubt that I thank the great authorities for their blessings. I am married to a human being who is a strong woman, with a deep understanding of human nature and the ability to deal with the particular and peculiar demands of a life revolving around music.

You see, my family had heard of another family that was looking to find a match for their daughter. My father sent a marriage proposal to the girl's family. While we were waiting for a response, my father heard that another young man's family had sent a marriage proposal too, with a very strong emphasis on the financial and extravagant gifts and funds that would be given to the couple upon marriage. Apparently, the girl's family was considering this proposal at the same time, and discussions were based entirely on comparing the monetary terms. My father immediately withdrew his proposal. I remember that he spoke to me about this. He said that though we could provide financial security, he was wary of people who looked at a relationship as crucial as this and saw only money.

I suppose it all boils down to the values that we grow up with, that we inherit from the generations that have come before us. This becomes the foundation, and upon this, we build our lives as we desire, or as God wishes it. Money has always had a place of respect in my life, because I have seen as much of what can be done with it as I have seen and experienced the stress of not having enough when you need it. However, money does not become more important than music, art, commitment, relationships and self-respect. I understand very well that this is easy to say, and when life throws hard times at you, nothing appears to matter as much as the lack of money. However, what you choose to sell, and what you choose to give for what you gain, are things to think about carefully.

I return to my dear wife. I have not said this to her as much as I should have, that she is dear to me. Amina is my cousin's daughter. We got married on 21 May 1960, when I was twenty-nine years of age. This marriage was arranged by our families amicably, joyfully and with a shared understanding of values.

I had accompanied my father when he had gone to her house with the proposal and strange as this may sound, coming from me, I did fall in love. At first sight. It is a little bit like being stopped unexpectedly by a completely unknown and invisible presence greater than anything you have known before. I know how that can happen because it happened to me. As it is with art, with music and poetry, there are times when you connect at the level of soul and spirit, and this is independent of knowledge or knowing, independent of time and of things explained or said. When this happens in a relationship, then it is the art, the poetry, the music of life itself. It is true that from such experiences have verses been written that would otherwise never have been composed. We forget upon reading, upon hearing the verse, that a human being felt something and lived that feeling so intensely that it poured forth with perfection.

What happened next?

The girl's family asked us for some time to think it over and get back to us. The truth is that this shook me to the core. I could barely hide my feelings from my family. Looking back at this younger me, I think I might have felt a twinge of hurt in my pride, which I might have hidden from even myself, thinking of the possibility that the family might actually consider refusing this proposal. Then that obstinate streak took over. Something in me knew that I would marry only Amina.

I understand it when younger people sometimes say these things and others around them put it down to the naturally romantic tendency associated with being a certain age. It has nothing to do with age. It has to do with absolutely certain knowledge. I have seen this repeat itself in the lives of my own children. I thank God that I lived and experienced my own life as I did, or perhaps I would not have had the capacity to understand or recognize this in another. I see it in my children; I have witnessed it with my own son Rabbani.

This period of intense moments of thought and feeling was thankfully cut short by the acceptance of our proposal by her family.

There it was. Life was good. I immediately re-focused on my riyaz. Not that I had ever stopped, but this was one of the few times in my life that something else occupied my mind so greatly. Later I came to know, to my great satisfaction, that Amina's family was very impressed with that one part of my life that meant the most to me—my music, my vocal skills, and they too wanted this match.

In so many ways, my life reflects that of my parents. My mother came from a tradition of music, understood music and needed no adjustment to the demands of this calling upon her family. I remember that out of an odd sense of concern, perhaps awkwardness, early in our marriage, when I did not know her as well as I do now, I had said to her, that if we were to become friends, she must never disturb my riyaz for any reason. She tilted her head and gave me a look that I can only describe as knowing, and deeply wise. For some reason I felt almost as if I should not have said this to her, that I should have known better. Well, perhaps, I should have known better than to explain these things to her. She has always understood the nature of musicians. She was born into a family with its own musical traditions and legendary singers—she is the granddaughter of Mushtaq Hussain Khan sahib, the first Padma Bhushan awardee of India.

Nobody knows how to run the home and routine of a family where music and riyaz always set the clock and the mealtime as well as Amina.

Ah. There I must catch myself again. Always is a strong word. Anybody who knows me well knows that I love the rains and I love the classic combination of pakoras and wet weather. Sometimes I am able to surprise those around me, and even myself. Ask Amina about rain and pakoras. She will laugh, and I know she remembers this one time when I was on a long trip, travelling for musical performances in the US. She was at home watching the hard monsoon rain outside the window. There is little you can do outside in the rain in Bombay. Perhaps two of the younger children were at home, but playing in another room. The rain can also make you feel lonely. That is when I rang the doorbell. The look on her face when she opened the door and saw that it was me was really worth cutting my trip short. I think she actually gave a little scream. She is really quite funny sometimes. The performances were done; I just had to cancel a few meetings to return to my monsoon and my home. As her eyes grew wide, I said, 'I heard you were making pakoras, so I caught a plane and came home. Am I on time?' She stared at me, her face breaking into a smile. 'Are they hot? Are you burning them?' I asked as I walked in.

I ate many pakoras that day, and not one was burnt except for the ones that were in the hot oil when I walked into the kitchen and asked her if I should try to fry one! What a fright she got! She shooed me out. Many years later, my little Shahina would try to make rotis, at my suggestion. A child making rotis has the most fun when they see how hard it is to get the round shape. I have eaten many different shapes of roti, all the result of Shahina's creativity. Sometimes she would burn them and get a scolding from Amina. It would cheer up the child when I would interrupt the scolding with a laugh and ask to try the rotis. I would tell her how tasty that burnt offering was and then Amina would give me a scolding. Sometimes I miss the joys of burnt roti shaped like a tiny little cosmic explosion on my plate. Children grow up too soon.

After we got married, we stayed in Badaun for a short while. I needed to resume where I had left off in my music and explained this to Amina. It seems unnecessary, in hindsight. I remember that she never made me feel uncomfortable about any of these conversations or decisions. She has always told me what she wants, and she has always let me go without a hint of constraint. I wanted to see what was happening in the music circles of Lucknow and Kanpur. All she said to me was that once I was settled and knew where I wanted to be, I should let her know so that she could join me there.

Living alone was no longer something I desired. I remember Amina warming up a meal and bringing me my plate, but seeing me engrossed in my riyaz, she would return the plate to the kitchen. I wonder if I ever told her about that fateful glass of milk at the Sangeet Dhara years ago. I am sure I did. I think that even if there were times when she felt a little impatient with my routine, she cared enough—she *cares* enough—to let me know that she understands how I feel. I wonder if I have been as understanding of her through these years.

Perhaps she thinks I have not noticed, but I have. She has patiently waited, many times, for over two hours until I have finished riyaz, so that she could reheat my food and bring it to me again. She would not eat either because she wanted us to eat together. In the times that I have lived alone, I have not bothered too much about my food. I would order in food from the local eateries nearby. The joy of eating homemade food together was important to me. Eating with Amina, with my family—this is happiness and contentment.

Food rituals are actually a very important part of life. I have always desired that my home and my table offer hospitality to a visitor. Sometimes, people would come home at odd hours, but Amina somehow managed, with enormous grace and affection, to make sure that everybody who came home was duly fed.

Not everyone will understand this. It is easy to dismiss it, saying that this is how it was for my generation. Yes and no. Sometimes people do things out of habit or because it is expected of them. This cannot mean that we underestimate the value of the actions which are done out of a sense of care and companionship. With Amina in my life, I have never felt lonely or alone again. Having experienced her presence in my life, I cannot imagine life without her.

God has blessed me in many more ways than one.

Music and Marriage in the Sixties

I packed a single suitcase and moved to Lucknow with my tanpura after my marriage. I stayed there for a few months but even my riyaz routine did not help me feel settled. I was looking for something else, a place where music and marriage could both find their home. I was about thirty at this time. Restlessness of a sort I had not experienced before overtook me. From Lucknow, I went to Kanpur. I met some old acquaintances as well as some new ones. I was invited to perform by a few people. Some of my old students heard that I had returned and they came to meet me. The word spread and more people requested me to teach them music. I found a place to stay in an area that was decent and I spoke to Amina to ask her if she would join me. She did, and that restless, unsettled feeling went away.

As the months passed, I realized that despite settling down both into my marriage and the music circuit in Kanpur, there was a sense of being in the wrong place. There was so much more happening that I, as a young man, was slowly becoming more aware of. There was a much larger world out there, in India and outside India. With radio and the increased interactions with others in music circles, I was hearing of new things. I heard of attempts being made by musicians to combine the elements of different kinds of music, but at that time, I was far too focused on my own music to spend time thinking about doing something like this myself. I had heard of Pandit Ravi Shankar working with musicians from other countries, introducing Indian classical music and our beautiful classical music instruments to audiences and musicians in Europe and the US (later, I learnt that he set up the Kinnara School of Music in Bombay in 1962, the same year that I moved to the city). Sometimes, I felt the odd sensation of being a tiny speck in a universe where mighty, unknown powers were shifting and creating new worlds. I remained resolute, my feet planted firmly upon the foundations laid by my father, my gurus and the greats of my gharana. It was only much later that I felt that if I continued to remain within the familiar confines of my own understanding of routine and riyaz in this small part of the world, where I had become so well-known, I would no longer be doing justice to my art, to my calling.

And so two years after we were married, Amina and I moved to Bombay. I made Bombay my home and have never stayed anywhere else after that. I remember seeing an airplane in the air for the first time in Bombay and was so fascinated by it that I told my relatives in Bombay that I wanted to travel in one. I do remember that they laughed at me. One of them, whom I shall not name here, mocked me. 'Go look at your face in the mirror,' he said. 'Your style is suitable for a bus, or maybe a train! Do you know the cost of a plane ticket?' I felt stung by these comments but kept quiet. I did not tell anyone, not even Amina at the time, though she heard this story later. Not everyone is pleased when one of their own begins to do well for themselves, or achieves something. Not everyone is happy to hear that one of their own has a desire for something beyond what they have. In life, I have learnt to stay away from such people.

I did not know then but my first ride in an airplane was to happen quite soon.

In the beginning, my three brothers, Amina and I stayed at the home of Ustad Hafiz Ahmed Khan, a relative of mine, who lived in Bandra. We were all so excited, moving to a major city from a small town in Uttar Pradesh. There was this feeling of anticipation—that my music would be heard by more people in a city where much more artistic and cultural activity was happening all the time.

Bandra then was nothing like Bandra today. It was not noisy with the sound of traffic, the houses were lovely, the environment was peaceful and neighbours knew each other well. There was a small nagging thought in my mind that I could not dismiss—that perhaps staying in the home of another person for too long was uncomfortable for all. I did not wish to impose on my kind host. I always wished to do things for myself; that is who I am.

Reluctantly, I raised the subject with Amina one day, perhaps abruptly. I told her I felt I needed some time to sort out a few things in this city by myself. I am afraid I have not always been gentle in the ways in which I have brought up difficult subjects. I know I tend to be blunt sometimes. All credit goes to her, though; Amina said that she too had been thinking that it was best that she returns to Badaun for a while until I had found my feet here. She said she had been debating whether or not, or even how, to say this to me, in case I misunderstood her. I have to admit I felt great relief upon hearing her and knowing that we were of the same mind.

Amina left Bombay in 1963. That year, thirty-two years old, I moved into a tiny paying guest accommodation at Cotton Green on the Harbour Line. The room was so small that only one mattress would fit in it. You may think it was brave of me to do this, and I think perhaps it was, but the truth is that I was hardly ever home. In addition, I did not have to worry about another person living there. I stayed busy travelling for shows around India, so the room was locked most of the time. It was, for me, just a place where I kept a few clothes, the place I returned to between performance tours to catch my breath, and then locked it to leave for the next tour.

Apart from these shows, I had begun to teach music regularly. I would go to the homes of my students and teach them there. My riyaz continued, as always, in my tiny room. Riyaz was never a problem for me and I sometimes practised through the night. I also occasionally went to the house of my friend, Ustad Shabbir Patel, to do my riyaz. He was a sarangi player. I continued to sing on the radio as well. Soon, I had an audience and a following all over India and abroad, who recognized my name and listened to my songs.

After Amina left in 1963, my travels included brief, joyful visits to see and be with her and the others in Badaun. They would ask me numerous questions about my travels and performances, the new encounters I had, and about my plans. I strove to organize my life so that I would be in a better position to make a home in Bombay with Amina.

I needed to leave that little room in Cotton Green. These things are easier said than done. As soon as I would return to Bombay, something else would come up. The tiny room continued to be the storage godown for my clothes and shoes and sometimes, for me.

Then things changed dramatically. On 26 January 1964, the country celebrated the fourteenth anniversary of the birth of the Indian Republic. President Dr S. Radhakrishnan, the great philosopher and teacher, Prime Minister Nehru, and a range of high-profile dignitaries, guests, and a large and enthusiastic public witnessed the parade. Thousands more across the country listened to the parade commentary over the radio. I can recall that Pandit Nehru unfortunately passed away the same year. There was, of course, no such thing as watching the parade on TV in those days. Though some people were speaking of this television business, nobody really understood it then—at least I, at the time, did not think of it as something that would gain the importance that it did over the next few decades. Jasdev Singhji had been the radio commentator at these Republic Day parades for years. He was there in the '60s. Namrata, who has been diligently exploring the history of these times that I recall through the haze of memories, tells me something interesting. Not only is Jasdev Singhji my contemporary, a Padma Shri and Padma Bhushan awardee, but it seems perhaps that he was born in the early 1930s as well, perhaps just a year separating us! She tells me that in a recent interview[1], he was asked how he

---

[1] Sidhartha Roy, 'The Voice That Put Life into R-Day Parades', *Hindustan Times*, 26 January 2013.

takes care of his voice and apparently, he said that he likes to eat pickles. I wonder if he has ever eaten a jar at a single sitting. I think I still hold that record. In this strange world, I find that more of us are connected in ways we will never understand, and that is why, when we speak to each other, the feeling of being strangers vanishes.

To return to my own little history, on this day, 26 January, we had a double reason to be joyful. Our daughter Nazma was born. Our first child, born in a free India, was born on Republic Day! Well. If you think marriage is a big step, let me tell you, the birth of a baby can shake you up and change everything overnight. That year, I decided my goal would be to bring my family to Bombay. No more Cotton Green.

Yet, Cotton Green was not done with me. In this same year, one of my big dreams became a reality in that tiny room.

Because of my radio performances that were heard outside the country, I was invited to East Africa to perform my music. So it was that I—with a face and a style meant for a bus—sat in an airplane for the first time in 1964. I chuckle as I write this. I sound like a child even to myself. You see, though I have never spoken in this way to anyone, certainly not to the person who had made that comment about me, I know that I cannot help but feel satisfied with the progress of my life. That is all I desire.

East Africa was my first trip abroad and my performances turned out to be a huge success. However, this was not how things began there! After I landed and reached the hotel, the organizer of the tour met me, his face clouded, as if disaster had struck. My first flight out, my first trip abroad, and I arrive to see someone in tears. This person was one of my students.

I asked him what had happened and he fell at my feet, he was so distraught. I calmed him down and finally got the story out of him. He said that after he had organized everything for the performance, suddenly, there was feedback from the circle of potential audiences that they were not interested in classical music. They were typical businesspersons, and as an audience, they had no experience or appreciation of traditional Hindustani songs or compositions. Apparently, they told him that his ustad may be a fine and well-known artiste in India, but here, nobody wanted to listen to his kind of music.

I thought about this and realized that I had to adapt to this situation and help a student of mine, who, out of the love and goodness of his heart, had done his best to organize and put this show together. I took a swift decision. I was already here. This was a good opportunity to expand the circle of appreciation of Hindustani classical music, among listeners who neither knew nor had the opportunity otherwise to hear our music traditions and styles. I told my student to cancel the auditorium but to plan smaller gatherings of people interested in music. I made a new performance plan and began to initiate these new audiences to our music in easy doses. I began with bhajans. They loved these. Word spread. The gatherings became larger. I added different kinds of music very slowly with each successive event. The audiences listened; they liked what they heard. They returned for more. I cannot tell you how much I enjoyed this experience. Such an incredible opportunity to build appreciation among people who only needed a little bit of handholding. Finally, I reached that level of performance with this now initiated audience that I sang pure classical music. I had listeners at the end of some of these performances who came up to me, laughing and happy, admitting to me that it was this technique I used, over this sustained period of time, that had gotten them to sit and listen to me singing khayal and other classical forms through the night!

Nairobi was also the country where I watched TV for the first time in my life in 1964. In fact, my performances were televised, so I did my first recordings in a TV studio and watched myself on TV! I remember this experience quite well. It was strange to see myself perform, strange also to think that so many others could see me sitting in their homes.

There was a large Indian diaspora there at the time, with strong ties to their home country, primarily for business and for marriage alliances. Music was a large part of the experience of connection and familiarity for this audience. I could feel a very different sense of being loved and appreciated, as much for my music as for the fact that I was part of the India that they cherished. You may leave your country due to different considerations or compulsions, but somewhere, the heart knows, home is home. I think this is true of everyone anywhere in the world.

I enjoyed the thrill and novelty of my tour experience in another country, while at the same time, the feeling began to grow in me that I am happiest in my own home.

After this trip, my international travel really began in earnest. Over the years, I have been invited to perform in many countries and I have embraced these experiences for all that they have had to offer. Yes, there are some stories I recall with more clarity than others. Before I come to those,

I need to get back to my Bombay, to my marriage, as much as to my music!

In 1965, two years since Amina went back to Badaun, I was reunited with her by the grace of almighty Allah. I found a nice place for us at Akram Terrace, which was behind the Mahim Makhdoom Baba Dargah. The entire family joined me here.

That year, in January, my daughter Shadma was born. A day before Republic Day! I was determined to share some of the responsibility of caring for this second child with Amina. I wanted to do the things I missed with Nazma in the previous year. Our lives are gifts from the Almighty. Our occupations are gifts and our relationships are gifts, all from the same source. Music, my occupation, my calling, received everything I could possibly give—my time, my energy, my discipline. My relationships on the other hand, I have always felt that I have not been able to give to as much as I would have wished. With Shadma, I learnt a little bit about what it is like to care for an infant. I could do little else in the first year but hold her in my arms when she was sleepy. It makes me happy to remember that when I did this, she would go to sleep almost immediately.

It is hard to think of these children as adults now, with lives and families of their own. For the longest time, I recall, I would follow my children around whenever I could. To the park. To school. Visit during break time. I wanted to see them grow, I wanted to watch over them. I did actually miss a lot of their childhood. I could not be two people or be in two places at the same time. Today, I know people have all these phones, live video, cameras and internet, so the world seems smaller and parents and children feel they can bridge the distance. Even distances between countries and continents. Skype, Papa, Skype, I hear my children say. Live, everything is live. I do not understand—how is it live when you are not there? Relationships are not supposed to be radio programmes. You cannot just broadcast yourself to your family to be together. You have to actually be together. That is of course not always possible, so I should not grumble. I have been grateful to technology for all that it has made possible in my life, my music and my relationships.

Still. I wonder still. About distances. Even if this technology of today were available to me in the '60s, how do you really think a voice on a phone or a face on a screen could take the place of these children? Living, breathing, wriggling, laughing, climbing trees, dropping things, making faces at each other when they thought we were not watching? I missed them when I was out for performance tours. When I was home, I may have been too much in their way sometimes, trying to make up for my absences.

Akram Terrace. Do you know who my neighbour was? The great tabla player, Ustad Allah Rakha Khan sahib. At that time, he was working with AIR Bombay and whenever he would leave for work, he would drop little Zakir at my house. Zakir Hussain was a little boy then, very smart for his age and full of energy! He would be everywhere at the same time, a real handful, you could not turn your head away for an instant lest you lose sight of where he was running to next. Ustad Allah Rakha sahib used to leave him with me in the hope that if he stayed with me, he would use his energy in doing riyaz with me. Zakir was a very sweet, naughty but super talented and intelligent child who learnt the intricacies of classical music very swiftly.

Many years later, while still in school, Zakir was to accompany me one day for another milestone in my life, the day I cut my first record. Not something either of us knew in 1965! It is only when you look back into the past, with the knowledge of all that has happened, that you are able to see the amazing and intricate pathways that God uses to bring people together. Actually, it was a milestone for him too—it was his first recording. I asked him if he would like to do this with me and I remember how his eyes widened and how swiftly he said yes. I had complete faith and confidence in him. I had watched him grow, practise and learn his art. The joy and focus I saw in him is something I recognized, as it sits deep within me too when I practise and when I perform.

So to return, as always, to my riyaz. In Bombay too, I used to practise for hours together and barely sleep for two-three hours in every cycle of twenty-four. Amina was pregnant with our third child. She used to get terribly bored because all she could do at the time was cook food. She had to stay at home the whole day. I noticed that her usual calm cheerfulness was both a little less calm and a little less cheerful. I saw in her a feeling of loneliness. Something had to be done. It is not enough to just have a person share your home with you, they must be happy too.

I wondered about what to do, but realized that unfortunately, all that I really knew was how to play music, compose music or sing.

Then I thought of something.

'Would you,' I asked her one day, 'like to learn how to play the tanpura?'

That was how it began. She said yes immediately. I felt strange that for all of her lifetime, this was one thing that had never happened before, surrounded as she was by music and musicians before her marriage, and then married to a singer and musician. So the lessons began. She took to them very well. I realized, as I told her, that with her learning the tanpura, she could help me too, keeping me company during riyaz and playing the tanpura.

At this Mahim house, in 1967, was born our third child, Murtuza, yet another January child, and this one born on the first day of the year. I wondered when I heard him cry whether one day he would sing. Would I, disciple of my own father and my gurus, teacher of students who came to me to learn music, would I one day be teacher to this baby that wailed so loudly that he could be heard in Badaun? Would he, in the years to come, accompany me to a performance, would we sing together? Oh, yes. Life was changing swiftly and now I had to keep pace with it on many fronts.

While we were still at Akram Terrace, Ustad Hafeez Ahmed Khan, who was at the time Director, AIR Bombay, was transferred to Delhi. His house in Bandra fell vacant. Hafeez bhai asked me if we wanted to move into his house and I gladly accepted his offer.

Bandra was beautiful, isolated and more like a village. This had its own disadvantages, which reared their heads soon enough. I did my riyaz in the night because of the calm at the time. There is no disturbance. The night offers peace for riyaz and *ibaadat*.

Unfortunately, my night-time riyaz irked my neighbours. This was becoming a part of my life. I almost became used to this, no matter where I lived. Things became bad here as well. Unbelievably, neighbours started throwing stones at my house whenever I began doing my riyaz. I tried to make light of it and would ask Amina whether she thought it was my singing that irked them, or the hour that I chose, or perhaps the volume. Amina was not amused. Having people fling stones at your house is a stressful thing to live with. My Padma awards were still quite a bit distant in the future and nobody, least of all me and my neighbours, knew that I was going to receive any of them!

Today, from the same Bandra, from some of those same stone-throwing neighbours, I have received letters of praise, congratulations and good wishes for my Padma Vibhushan. In these letters, some ask me if I remember them. They tell me they are proud that I was once their neighbour. When you reach the age that I am, life gives you many opportunities to chuckle.

Our fourth child, Qadir, was born that year. The last of the children of the '60s. Of course, that is not how I think of them. They coined that phrase for themselves many years later, these older ones, when they would have mock debates with the younger ones. This was also a very busy phase of my music career. I return to this thought, and to the regret that I could not spend as much time as I would have liked with my children when they were infants. I do not always remember the milestones other parents do—the first tooth, the first time one of them rolled over, or crawled, the first attempt to walk. The first word. And all the strange words they could not pronounce when they were learning how to speak!

Yet, I did the best I could, and all of my children have loved and supported me, they have been everything I could ever have wished for. They know, too, that they are precious to me, each one of them.

So, this music and this marriage, they were both meant to be as they are. The two halves of a full life. God's greatest gifts to me.

* * *

That decade of the '60s was a very busy time. Between settling into marriage and exploring the opportunities to widen my music and performance base, I think the years went by very fast. I do remember some tales from those days, such as the time I lost my voice just before a performance.

Here is what happened. I was travelling with other musicians by train for a show in Madras, as it was called in the early '60s. It was a long journey from Bombay, a distance of well over a thousand kilometres. When the train stopped at one of the stations, one of the musicians asked me whether I would like to have a medu vada. I was not hungry, but since he was asking me with so much affection, I told him I would. A medu vada is a fried snack and it is accompanied by coconut chutney. After eating this, I realized, to my utter horror, that I was unable to speak. I had almost immediately developed a throat infection. This was one of the dangers of travel—eating the wrong thing from the wrong place—and I was normally quite careful, having become a seasoned traveller by then.

All through the night, I remained worried and could hardly sleep. By nature I am not too much of a worrier, because I know that I do my best in any situation, and I have usually found a solution when a problem arose. However, sometimes, some things happen that are beyond our control and capability. This was one of them. I could feel a fever coming on. This did not worry me as much as the throat did. I have fought fever and performed before audiences and nobody has known, except of course in later years, when my sons have accompanied me. Then sometimes they know if I am unwell. Now, as the train rushed through the dark night, I wondered how I would be able to perform the next day with a throat like this. I told myself, with a heavy heart, that I would have to disappoint the audience by singing in a low pitch and would avoid singing in a high pitch.

The next day, I found myself on stage with a hall full of people waiting for me to begin. I was very nervous. I calmed myself and decided to do the best I could. Once I began, the familiar sense of being one with the music came upon me, and I know I forgot about my throat. At least, I know I stopped being so terribly conscious of it. Suddenly, I became aware in the gap between one piece and the next that everyone in the audience was clapping for me. I could feel that they were enjoying what they heard, they were happy to be here with me. I felt struck by a sense of disbelief. At the same time, immense relief and gratitude to God poured through me. I could not understand what was happening because according to me, I was not singing my best. I swiftly put these thoughts and feelings aside and continued with the performance. There was no room for distracting thoughts.

After the performance ended, many people came to me and said that they had never heard such renditions of some of the pieces I had sung as they heard from me that evening. They kept praising me even after I confessed that I had a sore throat and was not singing as I would have liked to. They did not believe me.

Later, I went to the greenroom, stood in front of the mirror and said to myself, '*Maine nahin gaaya. Allah ne gawaya. Agar maine gaaya hota toh har waqt main ek jaisa sound karta aur aaj bhi aise hi gaata* . . . (Today, it was not I that sang; today, God saved me from embarrassment. He was behind my singing. Had it been me alone tonight, my voice would have sounded the same through all the pieces, without variation of any kind).'

The Almighty does everything and he lets us take the credit. I have always felt this to be true, certainly in my life and in my relationship with music. In August 1965, Naina Devi had organized a concert in the memory of Mushtaq Hussain Khan, on his first death anniversary, at the Mandi House, New Delhi. She had been one of his students. A well-known singer herself, she would also produce music programmes for All India Radio, Delhi. I sang Raag Saraswati. As I was in the middle of this performance, I felt that I was no longer the singer, but that I was part of what I sang, that from somewhere beyond me, this music came and carried me through the performance. I remember that I also sang Raag Desh Malhar. After the performance, people came up to me with tears in their eyes and they applauded me. Yet, I know I felt that it was not I behind this music, it was God. I am really, and I have always been, just a person who is blessed to have this music find expression through me. All this applause and credit actually belongs to Allah. I think that each person who comes to listen as part of an audience is touched, personally and individually, by something in the music that connects to them. An audience is composed of hundreds of different people. For each to feel something so strongly is a gift from a much higher source than a human being is.

I remember another such story where divine intervention is the only way to understand what happened. The year was 1969, I think. I had a performance at Solapur in Maharashtra. The head of the women's social circle in Solapur, Chanchala Gandhi, had personally invited me to perform at a music event that their group had organized with great enthusiasm. Solapur was known to be a vibrant city, and art, culture and music had a strong place in the daily life of the people here. A Solapur audience was an audience that was already familiar and trained in the appreciation of artistic, poetic and music traditions. Artists such as Kavi Sanjeev, of multiple talents including poetry, sculpture and even photography, painters such as Almelkar, Sidram Jadhav who played the rare instrument called Sundari—they were well-known personalities from Solapur. Chanchala Gandhi herself was a singer, quite well-known at the time. So, you see, performing in Solapur was a significant event. There was a lot of publicity.

What happened was, as soon as I reached Solapur, I fell very ill. It started with a headache, and that is all I thought it was, until it got so bad I had to be rushed to the doctor. I had fever. His diagnosis was meningitis. The doctor told me to refrain from singing or exerting myself as the infection had travelled to my brain and the situation, according to him, was life-threatening. I do not know where or how I contracted this, but again, being a frequent traveller, there were health risks of all kinds. I do recall that in the '60s, meningitis was a health scare few of us were aware of. I did not even connect the initial symptoms, just a headache, with the possibility of a terrible illness.

When I told Chanchala Gandhi about this, she panicked completely, caught between worry for me but also anxiety because tickets for the performance had been sold, all in advance. It was too late to cancel or postpone now, one day before the show. There was a very strong possibility that the audience would not handle the disappointment well. Audiences have been known to behave much like a violent mob sometimes. When I realized how upset and helpless she felt, I decided I had to go ahead with the performance. I sang the entire evening, but I assure you, I do not know how I did so. The performance went by in some sort of a blur for me. It seems, however, that the music the audience heard delighted them, met and matched all their expectations. Again, all by the will of Allah. As the last song of the evening ended, the audience rose and clapped. I passed out on stage. Really, the next thing I remember is waking up in a hospital bed.

At the hospital, my condition was marked as an emergency and the doctors immediately operated on me. Amina rushed to Solapur to be with me. After twelve days of my being in the hospital, my younger brother, Aftab Ahmed Khan, brought us back to Mumbai. I was in acute pain and could neither stand nor sit without support. The pain was so bad that I had to sit the entire night in the train. Amina had to put pillows all around me to ensure that I did not tumble over. It is strange, though, that I felt no fear. Perhaps because I had my family around me, Amina with her strong presence, my brother readily organizing all that had to be done. Certainly because I have always believed that all that happens is as per the will of Allah.

Through all this pain and a body that seemed no longer to be my own, I knew how I had managed that Solapur performance. It is all thanks to God that I did not disappoint my audience or let down the organizers who had invested so much in the event. That was the only possible answer.

Divine intervention.

That explanation always holds true for everything.

Sometimes, it is about the help we receive, to continue despite pain and physical ill health. At other times, God carries us through challenging situations that are not obvious to others. They are not visible to someone looking at you. Such situations can be far more agonizing to soul and spirit. They demand from the human being an impossible strength and conviction. Such is the story of the time I had gone to Calcutta for a show.

I was doing my riyaz in my room to prepare for my recital when an organizer came to my room. He asked me what I was going to perform that evening.

I told him that I would be singing Raag Bageshri. He kept quiet for a minute, but I knew there was something he wanted to say. Until he had it out of his system, I would have him in my room, and my riyaz would be disrupted. That by itself is an unsettling feeling for me. As politely and as kindly as possible for me at the time, I asked him whether there was something on his mind. I could not believe it when he actually requested me to change what I was going to sing, to sing something else. I asked him the reason for his asking me to do so.

He hesitantly told me, 'Ustad Bade Ghulam Ali Khan sahib, who performed here last night, has already built the palace of Bageshri, the sound of which is still echoing here.'

Ustad Bade Ghulam Ali Khan sahib. The legend among the great names in all of the history of our classical music traditions. He was present at that performance of mine over a decade ago in Bombay at Babubhai Banker's mehfil, where I first saw him. It was Ustad Bade Ghulam Ali Khan sahib who had blessed me on that occasion, and I will always remember that he had said after my performance that I 'fully deserve to be called an Ustad'. His was the signature on that certificate! To attempt to sing something that he had already sung the night before requires a lot of courage.

Yet, that strange obstinacy, that part of my nature that raises its head ever so often, took over again. I did actually resent the tone of the person who was speaking to me. Something about it seemed to imply that I would fail my audience and myself if I sang what I had planned for today. That resentment turned into quiet determination. I would continue as I had planned. I told the young man, 'I don't care if my Bageshri is a mere hut in front of Khan sahib's palace, but I have decided that tonight, I will sing Raag Bageshri.' I looked him in the eye as I said this, and I saw in his face that he struggled to say something to make me change my mind.

I held up a hand to stop him before he could say another word. He took two steps back, thought better of things, then mumbled an apology. I nodded silently and he turned around and left. It took me a little time to compose myself. I wondered if I had taken the right decision.

It is unlike me to be so cut and dry, to refuse something directly, without even giving the other person a chance to speak further. Something within me felt that I had to stand up for myself because this person, by his attitude, was assuming he could put me down. This was a different way of bullying someone, insulting them. It was wrong. I would not accept this.

I sang Raag Bageshri that evening.

By the grace of God, the audience loved it.

Before the decade of the '60s ended, I crossed another milestone. I sang for my first Hindi film, *Bhuvan Shome*, directed by the well-known director Shri Mrinal Sen. Pandit Vijay Raghav Rao was the music director for *Bhuvan Shome*. He played the flute, was trained in classical dance, and was a poet—he was brilliant. I first met him during the making of *Bhuvan Shome*.

There were those in the circle of classical Hindustani music who had been lending their voice and art to songs in films for some time now. Ustad Amir Khan sahib had sung for *Baiju Bawra* with Pandit D.V. Paluskar. Ustad Bade Ghulam Ali Khan too, after great persuasion by Asif sahib, had sung for the film *Mughal-e-Azam*. Pandit Bhimsen Joshi had sung *Ketaki, Juhi, Gulab* for the film *Basant Bahar*. Pandit Jasraj of the Mewati gharana had sung recently, just a few years ago, for a film, a song called *Vandana Karo*. Hirabai

Barodekar, student of Ustad Abdul Wahid Khan sahib of the Kirana gharana, sang for the film *Pratibha* decades ago, as far back as the 1930s. Kishori Amonkar, born the same year as I, as Namrata informs me, just a month later—she too sang for a film in the mid-'60s. I was just a boy then, and certainly knew nothing of this world outside of Badaun, of films and of singers trained in classical music traditions who sang for films.

Well, that is how my life and music progressed.

It was a growing movement towards a direction that promised to allow more people a chance to appreciate music born of classical traditions. It was also a test and an opportunity for musicians such as me, steeped in those classical traditions. It asked of me that I step out of the known and the familiar world of radio programmes, concerts and mehfils to connect with wider and different audiences, some of them far less familiar with these traditions.

When I think of Papa's obstinate determination decades ago, when he somehow knew he would marry only her whom I call Ammi, I understand how he accepted the decision Rabbani and I were to take years later. Papa has experienced strong intent and determination within him his whole life. He is able to extend that experience to see how other people, his own son, then me, can determine the way we feel and stand by our feelings. He was brought up in a family where the elders are next to God. When the life decisions of younger members of the family were often guided, if not dictated, by elders, to decide any course of action by yourself, and within yourself, with obstinate determination, is a giant step in the direction of self-knowledge.

To live like this implies that you have a strong sense of who you are and what sort of a person you desire to be. He tells his stories of life in Bombay in the '60s and leaves out a very interesting fact. At that time, there existed a 'pagdi' system of housing, where a large amount of money is paid upfront as security by the tenant, with the actual monthly rent being nominal. Invariably, once a house was given out on rent, it became very difficult for the landlord to have it vacated. The tenant would go to court and say that since he had given a hefty amount as pagdi, on which the landlord had earned interest, besides the rent paid every month, he had paid the landlord enough money already to continue to live in the house. The tenant would file a plea saying that since he had no other place to stay, he should be allowed to continue to pay rent for the accommodation every month and be allowed to stay in it. When the issue became sub judice, the court would fix the rent until a decision was arrived at and would direct the tenant to deposit the rent in court every month. This left the landlord no way of either increasing the rent or getting the tenant to vacate. Such cases usually dragged on for years and the poor landlord would ultimately be left with no option but to sell his house to the tenant at a ridiculous price, much below the market rate.

When Papa talks about his days in Bombay and his taking up accommodation on rent in Mahim, we are not told of the part where, against the advice of the agent and his lawyer, he insisted that a lease deed be drawn with the terms and conditions clearly mentioned in it. He was protecting the *landlord, so that whenever his landlord wanted him to vacate, he would simply and without any worries have only to give appropriate notice, refund the security deposit (pagdi) and have him vacate his premises.*

Simplicity, integrity and honesty are at the core of Ustad Ghulam Mustafa Khan.

Children of the Sixties

Nazma

Whether or not I would have remembered this on my own, my father ensures that I and everyone else in the family will always remember that when I was a child, I could not say 'taxi'. Until today, Papa will lovingly, and embarrassingly, call out to me, 'takshi-takshi'! That, I assure you, is not my name!

I am Nazma Khan, the first child of Ustad Ghulam Mustafa Khan and Amina Khan. You ask me to talk about Papa. The first and foremost thing that defines him is that he is a very caring person. This quality has always been there, and it is not something that only we, his family, have known and experienced. Over the years, I have heard many people, including his students and others who have worked or collaborated with him on programmes and music projects, speak of him thus. This is the first thing they all notice and remark upon. It is a rare quality in a world where most people do not have the time to care about others.

One of his small acts of care I remember is when he would invite our friends home to meet them. He was affectionate and kind with them all, but as I grew older, I realized this was also his way of staying in touch with us. He ensured that we were keeping good company. Our friendships were with children from different kinds of homes and families, but one thing that was common to us all was a strong sense of right and wrong, good manners and respect, especially in our behaviour with elders, in our own family and each other's families too.

I also remember that there were times when he would be out for shows and performances for extended periods, when I would hardly catch a glimpse of him. I used to get very upset. I used to get even more upset because the little while that he was at home with us, he would seem to spend more time pampering my younger sisters and brothers. Well, I may be the oldest, but a child is a child and being the oldest does not mean you do not feel the need to be pampered. Somehow, he would immediately see the look on my face and respond to it by asking me things that I had been doing, telling me stories of his trip and giving me the attention I wanted, before I could ask for it! I will always remember that there were occasions—especially if he knew one of us was very upset due to his absence—when he would not take up shows for a few days so that he could be with us. Very few people can say this about their fathers, that they put work aside more than once because their children wanted to be with them.

Even today, despite his age, his caring nature surfaces at all moments. We see him with our children as a grandfather, and it reminds us of the times we were children, because he gets them to behave the same way he got us to listen to him! He will hold them and rock them to sleep, as he did with us. He does not like any of his children or grandchildren to be uncomfortable in any way. Sleeping, sitting, eating, travelling—he has always made sure we were fine. The only difference now is that he has more time to spend with his grandchildren than he had earlier, to spend with us. I do not hold that against him; I cannot, because he has made up for that lack of time over the years in a thousand different ways, to each of us. He is not one of those remote, distant people. He is emotional and affectionate.

Ustad Ghulam Mustafa Khan with his father, Ustad Waris Hussain Khan, wife, Amina Begum, and children

Ustadji and Amina Begum at Bara Imambara in Lucknow

Ustad Waris Hussain Khan

Ustadji at a performance in Mumbai

Ustadji performing at Radio Sangeet Sammelan in Varanasi, 1985

Delhi, 1952. From left to right: unknown, Hafiz Ali Khan,
Ustadji, Nissar Hussain Khan, unknown, Mushtaq Hussain Khan,
unknown, Kanthe Maharaj, Pandit Ravi Shankar, Jnan Prakash
Ghosh, Ali Akbar Khan, Radhika Mohan Maitra, Vilayat Khan,
Kishan Maharaj and Karamatullah Khan

Ustadji at a performance in Nairobi, 1964

Ustadji (second from right) with Pandit Nikhil Ghosh (far right) and
Ustad Bade Ghulam Ali Khan sahib (seated in the middle), among
others, after a recital during Sangeet Mahabharati's tenth anniversary
programme at Birla Matushri Sabhaghar, Mumbai, September 1966

Ustadji with Naushad sahib at a concert in Mumbai, 1968

Ustadji and Hariharan (second from left)
at a performance in Mumbai in the 1970s

A rare picture of some of the greatest Indian classical musicians, with former president of India, Rajendra Prasad (in the middle), taken during the first music conference of independent India in 1948. Ustadji was only seventeen years old at the time

Front row (from left to right): unknown, Ustad Nissar Hussain Khan (vocal), Ahmed Jan Thirakwa (tabla), Hafiz Ali Khan (sarod), Mushtaq Hussain Khan (vocal), Omkarnath Thakur (vocal), Rajendra Prasad, Kesarbai Kerkar (vocal), Baba Allauddin Khan (sarod), Pandit Kanthe Maharaj (tabla), Pandit Govindrao Barhanpurkar (pakhawaj), Pandit Krishnarao Shankar Pandit (vocal), Pandit Anant Manohar Joshi (vocal)

Second row: Ustadji (vocal), Ustad Altaf Hussain Khan (tanpura), unknown, Karamat Hussain Khan (tabla), Pandit Radhika Mohan Maitra (sarod), Ilyas Khan (sitar), Ustad Bismillah Khan (shehnai), Kishan Maharaj (tabla), Ustad Ataf Hussain Khan (vocal), Pandit Ravi Shankar (sitar), Ustad Ali Akbar Khan (sarod), Ustad Vilayat Khan (sitar), Pandit Narayanrao Vyas (vocal), Pandit Vinayak Rao Patwardhan (vocal), Pandit Dattatreya Vishnu Paluskar (vocal)

Third row: first five people are from Ustad Bismillah Khan's party, Professor B.R. Deodhar (vocal), Pandit Jnan Prakash Ghosh (tabla), Rajyadaksh (vocal), unknown, unknown, Nimkar Bua

Fourth row: unknown, Vinaya Chandra, Pandit Gajananrao Joshi (violinist and vocalist), unknown, unknown

Ustadji with former president of India,
Gyani Zail Singh, at Goa governor house, 1984

Ustadji performing with his guru, Ustad Nissar Hussain Khan
sahib, and his cousin Ustad Hafeez Ahmed Khan

Ghulam Ali Khan sahib with Ustadji after a performance in New Delhi

Ustadji with Shaan

Ustadji with Lata Mangeshkar and Gulzar (in the background)

Sonu Nigam at Ustadji's residence for the Ganda Bandhan
ceremony, as per *guru-shishya parampara*, 1996

Ustadji and Sonu Nigam during the former's eighty-seventh
birthday celebration at The Club in Mumbai

Ustadji performing at the Souls of India concert in Jaipur

From left to right: Ghulam Murtuza, Ustad Zakir Hussain, Hariharan,
L. Shankar, Ustadji and Vikuvinayak Ram, after a performance in Mumbai

Ustadji with Shivkumar Sharma (far left), Pandit Jasraj (second from right) and Anandji Virji Shah, October 2016

Ustadji being honoured on his seventy-fifth birthday by Pandit Ram Narayan. Also in the frame are (from left to right) Ustad Amjad Ali Khan, Ram Shrivastav and Hariharan

Ustadji being awarded the Padma Shri by former president of India, R. Venkataraman, in New Delhi, 1991

Ustadji receiving the Sangeet Natak Akademi Award, 2003, from A.P.J. Abdul Kalam. In the same frame are Jaipal Reddy and Sonal Mansingh

Ustadji being awarded the Padma Bhushan by former president of India, A.P.J. Abdul Kalam, in New Delhi, 2006

Ustadji receiving the Dinanath Mangeshkar Award from Lata Mangeshkar
in Mumbai, 2011

Ustadji being awarded the Padma Vibhushan by President Ram Nath Kovind in
New Delhi, 2018

Ustadji with Prime Minister Narendra Modi at Rashtrapati Bhavan after receiving the Padma Vibhushan

Ustadji with Home Minister Rajnath Singh at a dinner party hosted for Padma awardees in New Delhi

Ustadji at Rashtrapati Bhavan with other Padma awardees

Ustadji with L.K. Advani in New Delhi, 2018

From left to right: A.R. Rahman, Namrata Gupta Khan, Rabbani Mustafa Khan, and Ustadji (in the background)

Ustadji with Hariharan, Sonu Nigam, Namrata Gupta Khan and Shaan at a wedding in Mumbai, 2018

Ustadji with Hariharan

Ustadji with his brothers—Ustad Aftab Ahmed Khan (left) and Raza Hussain Khan—in Mumbai, 2018

Ustadji with his younger sister Zakiri Begum in Mumbai, 2018

Ustadji with Amina Begum in Mumbai, 2018

Ustadji and his family on the wedding of his grandson, Shiraz Ali Khan

From left to right: Ustadji with his sons, Qadir Mustafa, Rabbani Mustafa, Hasan Mustafa, Murtuza Mustafa, and grandsons, Aamir Mustafa, Zain Mustafa and Faiz Mustafa, in Mumbai

I know what it means when a person is a pillar in the life of those around them because of my father. My father has always been, and remains, a strong pillar in my life, always standing beside me in difficult times. He has said sometimes that he missed time with me, the first-born, that staying apart for that period of time when he lived in Cotton Green and we were in Badaun, was hard for him. I have no memories of the time, I was an infant. What I do remember is how he has been an integral part of my childhood and my growing up years.

I look at the world as it is, at the lives of so many around me, I see parents and children who do not get along, or who have severe problems with each other, and I know that I am blessed to have been born into this family. The one thing that we are is that we are strong together. That makes each of us confident in our own ways.

* * *

Shadma

I am Shadma, Ustad Ghulam Mustafa Khan and Amina Begum's second child. Like Nazma, I too am January-born—in fact, just one day before her, though one year after.

I believe that in my entire family, I have been the closest to my dad. He would rock me to sleep when I was a baby, feed me with his own hands, and even bathe me when I was a little child. I suspect this made my older sister Nazma feel a little upset sometimes—when we were younger, of course, not now.

The world may or may not know this, but we know it, that to Ustad Ghulam Mustafa Khan, his family is of utmost importance. I do not remember him having even a single meal without us when he has been in town. When he would sit to eat, he would first feed all of us with his own hands and only then begin eating. This kind of love becomes a part of your soul. I think it made us who we are.

Yes, he travelled a lot. Even when he was in town, I cannot say he was always with us, because there were shows, meetings, recordings and his music classes. The week would fly by and we would not see him much. Sundays were special. Every Sunday was family time for him and he would take time off his busy schedule and take us around the city. One of my fondest memories of family outings was the annual Makhdhoom mela. This is a fair that celebrates and honours Hazrat Makhdoom Shah Mahimi, a Sufi saint who is revered by many. His dargah is at Mahim. The mela is a few hundred years old, I think. It takes place on the beach at Mahim, behind the timber market. It was very exciting for a child, and also overwhelming. There were joyrides, all sorts of delicious food, there were stalls with toys and games, and many people came on each of those ten days of the fair. I was terrified of cameras, but he would still insist on getting pictures taken of us, as he believed in making memories and preserving them for posterity.

Whenever he was home, he would drop us to school in a 'takshi' (as my sister Nazma used to pronounce it when she was a child) and he would also visit us during the recess. However, as we grew older, that got a little embarrassing for us. I remember when he would come to see me at the gate, my friends would tease me. Initially I used to ignore them, and sometimes I would laugh as I ran to the gate. But I felt a niggling unhappiness about being teased. I think I remember feeling a little irritated that my father would do this when other fathers did not!

'Eh, Shadma, your father is here.'

'Run fast! He's come to check on you!'

'He's making sure you're attending class!'

'Are you getting extra tiffin?'

Finally, it became too much for me. I went home crying one day and asked him, 'Papa, *kya aapko humare upar bharosa nahi hai*? (Papa, don't you trust us?)'

Tears came to his eyes when he saw my tears and he replied, 'Beta, *mujhe tumhare upar bharosa hai par mujhe* Allah *ko muh dikhana hai ki apni* duty *sahi de raha hun* (Daughter, I have full trust in you, but I have to face Allah one day and let him know that I have performed my duty as a father to the best of my ability).'

That he has done and continues to do. As children, there are many things we do not understand and realize. He has been the best father one can ask for, always catching up with whatever was happening in our lives. Actually, it is more than just catching up. With Papa, it is never just about asking what is happening in our lives since the last time that we met or spoke, even if it was just yesterday. It is about knowing how we are feeling and doing, knowing how life is affecting us. I cannot recall a single time that he sat with me to catch up and was distracted by something else, or paying me partial attention.

Papa also has a great sense of humour. One night, when I was just about twelve years old maybe, I was lying next to him but could not fall asleep because I was scared of something. I do not even remember now what it was, but I had heard something from one of the other children in school. Some silly story it must have been of ghosts or unknown monsters. Whatever it was, I was scared to shut my eyes and equally scared of keeping them open in case I saw something! I shook him and woke him up, saying, 'Papa, *mujhe darr lag raha hai* (Papa, I am feeling scared).' He woke up and initially tried to calm me down and put me to sleep, but in the process, fell asleep again. I was still scared and woke him up again! This happened so many times that finally he got up and pulled a very scary face at me. All

I could see were his eyes, his flaring nostrils and his teeth! Horrified, I screamed. Immediately, he felt terrible, sat up, and put a hand on my head, and with the gentlest voice, he said he would stay awake and make sure to watch over me while I slept. I did sleep. I also remember that until I actually fell asleep, I pretended to sleep just to check on him once or twice. All of the times that I looked at him from beneath half-shut eyelids, he was sitting up, awake, I could feel his hand on my head, his other hand holding mine. I slept.

Yes, my father had a busy schedule, but he always made sure that he was there for us in many different ways. While touring abroad for months, he would write to Ammi regularly and ask her about us. Then, when telephone service started, he would call us on the MTNL landline of Sunrise Irani Hotel (the hotel in our neighbourhood), and Ammi would take us there, where all of us would stand in a line, waiting to hear his voice. These are things you never forget. They are the events of my childhood.

Growing up, I was always very interested in what my father did. I used to follow him around wherever I could and in fact, I think I may have learnt how to crawl for the first time trying to follow him from one room to another! As I grew a little older, I would go around with him, attend his concerts with him and find out everything about his schedule. He never discouraged me; he never showed impatience with me. I imagine it is not easy to have a child always hanging on to you, wanting to go with you everywhere. He always encouraged my involvement in his work. He was the one who taught me how to write letters, and by the time I was thirteen years old, I was writing letters for him. He insisted though that I learn how to communicate in a way that was both gentle yet professional. I learnt from my father, because he is this kind of a man, that it is important not to hurt people's feelings or their pride.

He used to bring me many gifts, mostly dresses, and I used to feel like a princess. Of course, this reminds me of another little story, when I was much more grown up. It was about clothes. It was a hot summer afternoon. You know what Mumbai is like in summer? Hot, sweaty, terribly uncomfortable. The humidity can be unbearable. Papa was roaming around the house wearing shorts. I was cooking in the kitchen and when I came to the room in which he was sitting to get something, he suddenly looked up at me and asked me to wear a dupatta.

I told him, 'Papa, *aap khud toh garmi ki wajah se* shorts *pehenke ghum rahe hain, hum dupatta kaise pehenein* (Papa, you are roaming around the house wearing only shorts because of the heat; how do you expect us to wear a dupatta?)' He just looked at me, frowned, then nodded as if realizing something, and said nothing after that.

He would always encourage and support me. He was proud of the fact that I did well in school and college. Four years after my graduation from college, I was busy around the house with some chores, when he suddenly came up to me and asked, 'BEd *karogi* (Do you want to do a BEd)?'

I just looked at him and said, 'Ji, Papa (Yes, father).' This was a big moment. To study further, to have my own father open the door to such an opportunity, was unheard of in my circle.

No sooner did we have this brief exchange than he asked me to stop whatever I was doing and get dressed. I did. We went together for my admission and so I enrolled into a BEd Course.

In 1993, when Mumbai was witness to communal riots, my parents would take a taxi together from our house in Bandra to my college, making me sit between both of them. They would leave the house during those disturbing days only so that I could attend my classes. This was a time of mobs, of violent crowds, of police firing; you could not foretell what would happen next and where. We have lived through troubled times. Later, it was reported that almost 900 people died in those riots. My father was past sixty years old then. We have never felt afraid or insecure because he and my mother have always been there, holding our family together, doing whatever was necessary to take care of us, because to them, we remain children. To be looked after. Even today.

* * *

Murtuza

Ustad Ghulam Mustafa Khan sahib is my father and my guru. There is a phrase, 'friend, philosopher and guide', and I understand it personally because it perfectly describes the relationship I have with him. He is the pride of my life.

I am lucky to have Papa as a guru because he is the teacher every student wishes and prays for. He was born to teach. Not everyone can be a teacher as it takes skill and a special wisdom that is much more than knowing the subject that is being taught. He excels at both. You may feel that I praise him because he is my father. Yes, that is a very good reason, but it is not the whole reason. I am not the only one he has taught, and several other of his students will agree with me. It is not just about the music—there is something about the man that makes the experience of learning from him very special. As a guru, he is like a parent, or as they say, 'in the place of a parent', for all his disciples. I am fortunate to have him as both, my guru and my father. To me, as a guru, he has been a loving but strict teacher, a disciplinarian. As a father, he has been the best that a child could ask for.

My memories of childhood, at least the very early years, are not very different from that of my older sisters', actually.

He travelled a lot. We missed him a lot. When he was at home with us, he would be 100 per cent present! I have seen people who stay at home. I observe they lead lives like clockwork, spending time at home every day. Not all of these people have given thought to the value of home or the others who are a part of that home. Then it becomes almost natural that the children grow up without giving value to their home. We learn from what we see and experience, don't we? I saw our parents and the way they lived, as did my brothers and sisters, and we grew up together in an atmosphere of deep love and respect for each other and for home.

I have thought a lot about why my parents held our family together as they did. I think the reason is that when my father and mother got married, the early years were not easy for them. They were unable to stay together for long periods. I know about these things, as do my siblings, because our parents have always told us about their lives and the things they value. They have not hidden things from us. My father is not a great talker, in the sense that he may not have long conversations with you, but it is the way he is, the things he does, that tell you what kind of a man he is. The way we experienced him, we always knew we were important to him. His being away did not ever mean that he was not present as a father.

We were in awe of him as we were growing up and learnt that many others were in awe of him too. However, as very young children, we only knew him as someone who loved us dearly, cared for us, and did not think twice about doing all sorts of things for us! I think the discipline of riyaz that he instilled in us from a very young age was much more than a discipline for learning music. It taught us a way of being. We learnt to focus; we learnt how to be persistent and to sustain our efforts.

I remember how much fun we had when he was not travelling, not working and spending time with us, especially the Sundays. He would make it a point to have family outings for the day and there was always some part of the day's plan that was important to each of us individually. Each of us felt satisfied with the day's doings. He would drop us to our school on the mornings he was in town. He did this even if he was tired and had come home late the previous night.

My father is a person who is clean of heart and pure of soul. Of all that he has seen and experienced, good and bad, nothing has left a negative mark on him. He has no bitterness towards those who have ever wished or done him ill, and he has no ego or false pride as a result of the adulation that has come his way. A more balanced and steady human being would be hard to find.

I believe Papa has worked very hard and given himself to every relationship he has had, starting with his parents, his gurus and his music. He has been a good student and disciple of his gurus, a good guru to his own students, a good son to his father, a good father to his children, a good husband to his wife and a good brother to his siblings.

Of music and him, there is nothing more that I can say— his whole life is proof of his commitment to that relationship. That is his biggest legacy to us.

* * *

Qadir

I will always remember being eleven years old, because something very important happened at that age. I was doing riyaz with my Abba (grandfather), unaware of the fact that Papa had arrived and was standing in a corner, listening. He was so pleased to see how well I was progressing that he decided to take me with him for his performances.

I am the fourth child of Ustad Ghulam Mustafa Khan and Amina Begum, born in March 1969. I guess one dynamic of my relationship with my father, which has been a constant all my life, is that of guru–shishya. He has been an inspiration and teacher to me, not just in music but in every aspect of my life. Everything I have learnt has come from observing him and how he is as a person.

I grew up watching my father at the peak of his career. Although the interest in music was inherent, it was his success that became a motivational force, pushing me to learn music and start singing. He too wished for his sons to accompany him on stage. All our wishes seemed to be in alignment.

Being at the peak of his career, touring all over the world, he could not give us all his time in the initial years of our training, so we learnt under our grandfather, Ustad Waris Khan sahib. We followed our father's steps here, unknowingly so. It is a small but interesting fact that my grandfather, during our practice, said how we were just like our father when he was a child! I know that nobody but my brothers and I have had the joy and honour of experiencing this, to stand before my grandfather, reflecting our father's image.

I began to perform with my father at a very young age. In the initial years of these performances, I remember being intimidated and awestruck, afraid to sing next to him. My father sang effortlessly, making the most complicated sections seem so easy. I recall this one time when I was afraid to go on stage with him. He knew when to be kind and easy on us, but he also knew when to push us, and in fact, he knew exactly what worked with each of us. With me, he insisted that I perform, saying '*Agar tum ne baith ke awaaz nahi lagayi toh stage pe hee maarunga* (If you just sit there and do not sing, I am going to whack you

right there on stage)!' This was enough to get me going. I
sang. The thought of being whacked in front of everyone was
intolerable. As children, we are conscious of the world around
us and particularly of how we appear to others. In my case, I did
not want to appear frightened or anything less than the son of
this man! Do you notice how pride can be a great motivator?
My father knows these things. That is what makes him a great
teacher. He will not allow our fears to get the upper hand. We
learnt this young, and then we learnt from him how to handle
these fears for ourselves.

Soon after this incident, he started taking me all over India
with him. What unforgettable experiences these were! The
exposure and understanding I received, as did my brothers,
from such a young age, are all part of the training we have been
blessed with. I saw with my own eyes what happens before a
performance, how preparations are made, and also that often,
despite all the planning and support, things can happen that
can throw the show out of gear—what to do then, and what
the responsibility of a performer to the audience is. My father
always discussed things with us, he explained things to us. It is
from him that I have learnt that no matter what goes wrong or
right, it is how we are and the spirit that we project at that point
that makes all the difference.

My first international tour with him was in 1987, to
Pakistan. I was just about eighteen at this time. I went to
many international performances with him. I remember that
the show was a great success and the audience responded to us
with great enthusiasm. I also remember that there was some
problem with the organizers and with payments. My father
has never made money his priority. As I saw him speaking to
people at the time, I realized that one of the most important
things about him is the pure place he keeps in his being for
his music. Money matters, one way or the other, have not

interfered with his approach to music, performances and audiences. This is very unusual in the world we live in today—it is not impossible to find such a person, but it is difficult. To be truthful, there are times I have wondered if it is impractical to take this approach. It always comes down to the man; this is him and that is all there is to it.

By the age of twenty-three, I started performing solo all over India. We would talk every day over the phone. This strong connect that we maintain is at the centre of all that I do. I know that skills and abilities can be learnt, practised and honed, but there is no substitute for the love and support of those who wish you well. These are the real blessings.

I never felt that my effort would go unrewarded in the long term, even if I had a setback or disappointment of any sort in the short term. I think he has taught us to accept that life has many moods and moments, not everything is about immediate success. You see, his insistence on riyaz has many other consequences, apart from trying to achieve perfection through practice. I learnt that underlying the discipline of riyaz is the discipline of standing your ground, doing what you are meant to do, and doing it consistently. It is not the world that has to be consistent. What you seek is within you.

When I was a child, I used to love cricket and was actually quite good at my game. Papa was quite strict about the use of our time and our schedules, and he did not let us waste time. Every afternoon, in order to keep us home, he would lock the main entrance to the house. He was also very innocent. Murtuza and I had our own ways of bypassing all this. When all was quiet, and he was resting, we would secretly, silently, escape by another entrance. He would often not come to know. Sometimes, though, he would! Then he would come looking for us, heading straight to the maidan (field) where we played. We would get a scolding. However, there were also those days when he would sit at the window, watching us play cricket on the road. I think that he had to discipline himself to discipline us, because I feel he understood the joy of being spontaneous and breaking the schedule. He rarely ever did this, though. The only times I have ever seen him behave with an unusual sense of freedom and delight is during the monsoons. That is definitely Papa's season. During the monsoons, we all got away with many things he would not otherwise approve of.

He is such an amazing father in a thousand ways. He did not just become friends with us, his kids, but also became friends with our friends. Whenever we were late to school, he would drop us to school in a taxi and would drop our friends too. If there were too many kids, he would still find a way to make room and we would all wriggle about and pile in on top of each other, squirming and creating a racket till we reached.

In 1999, I recorded my first song, *Piya Haji Ali*, for the film *Fiza*, as a playback singer with A.R. Rahman. My father was so happy when I made him hear it. This is an aspect of his personality that has helped us all. He is open to music and art in multiple forms—traditional, classical, a blend of both— and he is able to connect with the popular and the mainstream as well. That is not to say he accepts and likes everything. He has his personal taste in art and music, but it is reflective of a wide range of expression. So, with his blessings and training, I went ahead in my career as a playback singer, a guru and vocal coach, alongside training students like the Band of Boys, Armaan Mallik, Terrance Lewis, Elli Avram, VJ Andy and music director Geet Ganguli, to name a few. I was also a vocal coach for TV reality shows like *Indian Idol*, *Sa Re Ga Ma Pa Lil' Champs* and *India's Got Talent*.

His involvement in our lives has made us confident. We have always known that we have him to fall back on.

The stories and memories shared by my sisters-in-law and brothers-in-law have one striking thing in common—each of them feels special; each of them has grown up knowing that their dad loves and cares for them, and will stand by them.

There is a phrase that has done the rounds for years, and people write about it and discuss it in reference to relationships everywhere. The phrase is 'quality time'. The experiences I hear from the children of Ustad Ghulam Mustafa Khan bring to mind a completely different interpretation of this phrase. That all time can be quality time when a person is present in the relationship. It is not about being physically present or absent. It is not necessary for a person to come home every day and rock the kids to sleep for the kids to know that they are safe and loved.

Being present is a quality Papa has. This is one of the biggest reasons for the lasting impact he has on most people. He is present in his interactions with everyone, his riyaz, his music.

Papa has sung despite fever, with a throat infection, with other problems outside his control including, for example, having musicians of inadequate capability accompany his singing. His audiences at these performances have never known of the stress under which he has sung, because at no time has it affected his singing. There is more than expertise and experience involved here. As I heard and recorded his stories from the '60s, he casually spoke of a time he gave a performance while diagnosed with meningitis. I thought I had heard this wrong, so I had him repeat it to me with whatever details he could recollect. When he saw my open-mouthed look of disbelief, he smiled and said that sometimes, we are able to extend ourselves beyond our ordinary human capacity because something higher up, a power greater than us, keeps us safe.

Between the conversations that I have had with him, sometimes weeks or even a month has passed without my being able to settle him down to tell me more. He takes things in his stride, so much so that if I did not actively, compulsively, pester him with my questions, many of these stories would stay locked away in his mind, a part of a valuable history that we would never know. Events that appear to be milestones to us do not seem to be so for him. Perhaps it is because he is very strongly centred. He has the honesty to acknowledge those feelings, and then he sets them aside and gets on with what he feels he has to do.

I asked Khan sahib about singing in other languages. He remembers that the first time that he sang in Marathi, it was for All India Radio. While he does not remember much about this time, he told me an interesting story of when he sang in Marathi for film music composer Shri Snehal Bhatkar. The famous composer was keen that Khan sahib sing his composition for the film, but the lyricist, Mangesh Karpadegaonkar, was not confident that Khan sahib, hailing from the northern state of Uttar Pradesh, would be able to do justice to the Marathi language. He was insistent that Bhatkarji get someone else to sing the song, someone who spoke Marathi fluently. Bhatkarji held his ground and stuck to his decision. He refused to change the singer, being completely confident in his choice. He was adamant that only Ustad Ghulam Mustafa Khan would sing the song.

Khan sahib did not know any of this, he heard the story later. He practised with complete concentration, as always, and rehearsed the song with Bhatkarji; finally, it was time to go to the studio for the dubbing. As the lyricist heard Khan sahib, his emotions showed on his face—he could not hide his expressions of astonishment! Khan sahib, from Uttar Pradesh, sang as if Marathi was his mother tongue. Bhatkarji was immensely pleased, and doubly so, to have had his decision be proven right. The story came out because Mangesh Karpadegaonkar came up to Khan sahib, applauded his work and then confessed to him how he had expressed his misgivings to Bhatkarji. My dear father-in-law tells me this story with a laugh. He did not hold it against the lyricist; in fact, he says he was touched by the honesty followed by the praise, for Mangeshji told him nobody else could have sung the song as he did.

It is difficult to get these little stories out of Khan sahib. It is not that he forgets them; it is that he does not speak about himself much. He often does not realize that many of the interactions he has had with people have left a mark on them. Another story I heard from him is about a performance in Ahmedabad when a well-known music composer, Rasik bhai, requested him to sing his composition. Khan sahib heard the piece and appreciated it a great deal. He says that he remembers being immediately struck by the beauty of the composition. Khan sahib wrote down the words of the poem in Urdu and went ahead to sing it in his own unique voice and style.

He remembers a song called 'Mazaa suraat mazaa me praan uthala', which he sang in Marathi, and another song, 'Mori preet ramaiya shamdu, mora naina barso na', which he sang in Gujarati, both for the radio. The famous flautist and Padma Vibhushan awardee, Pandit Hari Prasad Chaurasia, also from Uttar Pradesh and born in Allahabad, was a staff artiste at All India Radio Mumbai in the '60s. He too was on official duty in Ahmedabad and he accompanied Khan sahib beautifully for the Gujarati song 'Mori preet ramaiya'. This song remains very popular in Gujarat and is still regularly played on All India Radio. Khan sahib sings this song in Gujarati and you would not even imagine that Gujarati is not the native language of the vocalist!

When I hear these stories, one facet of this man that reappears often is his capacity to enjoy and appreciate, as well as support, the efforts of others around him. Many artistes, including some novices, have come away after a meeting with him feeling stronger, more confident, and more importantly, feeling that they have been heard and respected, that their efforts have been acknowledged by one who understands effort and art both.

He has been quoted in an interview, where he speaks about his writing, as saying, 'Pahle ghaliyaat ko dil se mehsoos karta hoon, tab jaakar compose kar paata hoon, ho sakta hai yahi vajeh ho (I first feel the poetry from the depth of my heart and soul, and only then try to compose it. This may be the secret you wanted to know)!'

An essential element of Papa's approach to life is feelings and emotions. He is very intuitive and is always attuned to the feelings of another person, or of the people in a room. This is impossible to describe—it must be experienced to understand how he affects people. I think perhaps that it is his creative ability that renders him super-sensitive to the invisible things that many of us do not notice or understand.

I believe Ustad Ghulam Mustafa Khan is one of those people who lives his life with the same heart and soul that he puts into music, song and poetry.

When the decade of the '70s brought with it a changing approach and attitude within the music fraternity, when the old and dignified tradition of artistes appreciating each other's work began to collapse and fray, Papa was caught by surprise. Through this decade, his forays into film continued, following his work on Bhuvan Shome at the tail end of the previous decade. His fame and popularity were very high. The children of the '70s, my other sisters-in-law Shahina and Rabia, my brother-in-law Hasan, and Rabbani, whom I would marry a few decades later, were now born and completed the core members of this family. Papa had very firm roots in both his family life as well as his work. He refused to be shaken by the events of this decade, even though some others that he will not name actively and aggressively tried to dislodge him from the primacy he held in the world of music.

As Papa says, 'Talent takes us to a higher position in our career, but behaviour will help us maintain a high position in the hearts of others.'

This is 100 per cent true. He has never behaved in a manner that he would consider unworthy of himself, not even if the other person has behaved badly with him. This is his nature.

In addition, nobody has been able to dislodge him from the position of respect, love and affection that he holds in the many hearts that have supported and surrounded him and continue to do so.

The Seventies—and the Music Plays on

I shall begin with something I am quite proud of. In the '70s, All India Radio frequency was available in Kabul, Afghanistan, and in Pakistan, and I was invited to perform, along with the Kathak maestro Birju Maharaj, by the ICCR when King Zahir Shah of Afghanistan visited India. I was told that he had heard my recording on the radio and was a big fan of my music.

I realized quite suddenly that I was well on the way to becoming an established and well-known musician now. I was being sought out for programmes and music projects of different kinds. I thanked God for all the good things I had experienced over these past two decades. It was as if my path had been cleared for me and I had to simply trust and follow it.

Pandit Vijay Raghav Rao got in touch with me again soon after our work on *Bhuvan Shome*. This time, he wanted me to sing for his film *Badnam Basti*. I had enjoyed my experience of working on a film and certainly enjoyed the experience of working with him. I agreed without any hesitation. This was in 1970 or 1971. The great poet and writer Harivansh Rai Bachchanji worked on the music of this film; he wrote some lyrics and vocalized them as well. His son, Amitabh Bachchan, had been the voice, the narrator, in *Bhuvan Shome*, though I do not recall him personally from those days. I think, if you ask me about my feelings and observations about singing for a film, I would say that the most interesting part is when you need to understand why you must sing, what the song is meant to express. You cannot really do this without some understanding of the story, at least the important elements. Singing for a film is not the same as doing a live performance before an audience where you choose the flow and sequence, or adjust your music according to the audience and their sensibilities. While recording a song for a film, you do not really have a sense of connection with the audience. You have to connect with the story. You have to use your imagination a little bit and your feelings a lot.

Life had settled into a somewhat regular pace and routine, both personally and professionally. The children were growing up. Nazma and Shadma were in school. The boys were younger and began school later. Amina had grown used to managing them without me. I did my best to help her with them when I was at home. Shows and performances kept me busy. My students kept me busy. I had a sense of responsibility towards them. As a teacher, I would feel that if I did not give each student the best that I could of all that I knew, of all there is to pass on through teaching, I would be letting them down. I was not willing to do any injustice to their education under any circumstances.

The relationship between an ustad and a student, that is, a teacher and a student, is one of enormous trust and faith. It is very much like the relationship between a parent and a child. This does not depend on age, because it is not about age. One can be thirty, forty or fifty, and still be a child for one's parents. A teacher can teach students who are grown-up, mature adults, and in that relationship, there remains a responsibility that takes on the colours of parenting. This does not mean that the student is less or small in any way, just as parenting does not mean that children are lesser beings. The respect that is due to a parent or a teacher is equally due to a child or a student. It is expressed differently.

By then, I had developed a reputation as a teacher. This brought me immense satisfaction. Students from all occupations, from all backgrounds, would approach me, because they had heard by word of mouth that I was a good teacher, someone they could trust to teach them well. This made me feel blessed many times over. To be given the gift of music, then to be given the gift of being in such a place in your life that you are required to pass on that gift to others, along with the knowledge that comes with it, is the most wonderful thing.

Thus it was in the early '70s, that I met Waheeda Rehman for the first time. She was already a famous actor when she came to meet me and sought to learn music from me. She had worked with the truly well-known actors of those decades, in films that today are classics of Hindi cinema. I agreed to teach her. Initially, she could be a student of mine only for a very short while, and then she had to move to a different city. She spoke with great simplicity and has always had an enormous ability to concentrate on a task. She surprised me one day in 2001. I got a call from her. She had returned to Mumbai and asked me if I would teach her now. Of course, I agreed. Life takes us all in many different directions and there is always a right time for everything. We may not always know what that time is, but we should accept that life is so.

Concentration is crucial to learning music and those prone to distraction find it harder, sometimes impossible, to learn. I feel blessed that none of my students has been prone to distraction. They have all had enormous capacity for sustained focus, besides innate musical ability. Readiness to learn music also means the will and ability to concentrate.

In 1973, a German film director heard about my singing and purchased a large number of my records to listen to. After listening to my singing, he decided to make me an offer to play the role of Baiju Bawra and use my voice as his for the documentary *Rain Maker*. This was being made on the story of Baiju Bawra, set in the life and times of the Mughal emperor Akbar and of Tansen, one of the nine jewels of his court.

I accepted this offer with gratitude. It was an opportunity to step into the shoes of a legendary singer. My voice would be recorded as the voice of the great singer for posterity. The film was shot in 1973 at the Amer Fort, near Jaipur, Rajasthan, and was an unforgettable experience for me.

Nineteen seventy-three was also the year that Shahina was born. My third daughter, she was a tiny, wrapped up bundle of naughty gurgles from the time she was born. Her personality shone forth in her smile and in the many faces and expressions she pulled even as a baby. I remember thinking to myself that in the years ahead, she would be one of those children who is everywhere and doing everything at the same time. They keep you very busy. Quite right I was, too!

My sixth born, Rabbani, who arrived the next year, 1974, was, as a child, often the innocent partner in Shahina's many explorations of the world. The difference in age between the two of them being just a year, they spent their infancy learning and doing things together till Hasan was born in 1975. These three children formed a natural bond of their own since the others were older. When you are that little, a year makes a big difference and four years is a big gap. Yet, things change, and the gaps mattered less as the children grew older. With Rabia, the youngest, who was born in 1977, her natural disposition was such that it was impossible for her older siblings to leave her out of anything. She would be found at the centre of everything.

I have always enjoyed doing things with all my children, involving them in my life as much as possible and as much as they wished to be involved. In the mid-seventies, I realized that Shadma was excellent with letters and communication. She had the right sensibilities and used the right words to communicate with another person in writing. I began to teach her how to write letters for me, how to respond to mails that came for me. She picked this up very quickly and towards the end of the decade, at barely thirteen or fourteen years of age, she was my official letter writer. By this time, Murtuza and Qadir were also in school. Murtuza had begun showing an interest in music and I had begun to teach him. Watching his older brother, Qadir too would want to be a part of this music education. I felt very happy. I knew in my heart that the day was close when my children would sing with me, and we would perform on stage together.

It was in the '70s that I finally got the first telephone of my life. I remember I got it through special category, due to the kind help of Nargis Dutt. This telephone became the lifeline of communication between my family and me. It was the link between me and my children through those long periods of performance tours when I was away from home. Grateful as I was, and still am, that audiences loved my voice, there were very many times when all I wished to hear was the voices of my children. I waited for the time when I would call them and ask them for news of their lives, of school, of riyaz and of home.

It feels good to have your family with you through life. Aftab, my youngest brother, has been close to me and we understand each other well. This is particularly important when sometimes, the world shows you a hard side of itself. Of course, performing with your siblings has its funny moments. Once, Aftab was performing with me at Akola in Maharashtra. I think this was perhaps 1977 or thereabouts. Suddenly, as I was mid-song, I saw him reach out for my mic and take it away from me! I continued to sing, but stared at him, bemused. Then I reached out and took the mic back from him! I think I may have heard a small laugh or two from the audience. I think they were equally surprised. I looked at Aftab who realized what he had done, looked horribly embarrassed, and pointed to his mic, looking at one of the organizers waiting in the wings. Quickly, his mic was changed—the first one, it seems, had stopped working and without a second thought, my brother had reached out for mine! Looking back, these are funny moments—I told everyone at home what he had done, and I made sure he never forgot! Aftab was perhaps one of my first students, being my youngest brother. One story I have kept to myself all these years is a little secret of his that he thinks I do not know. As part of his training, I would tell him to listen to me during my riyaz sessions in the night. He would get sleepy at some point in the night and I would send him off to bed. The little fellow only pretended to go, but I knew he stayed hidden in the room, listening even harder. I let him be. I let him surprise me the next morning with all the extra things he had learnt the night before! He made me proud.

There was a time between the mid-seventies and the mid-eighties when there were many great artistes and performers of Indian classical music. Each was a master at their craft and highly respected by their audiences and patrons. I believe it must have been a boon for the lovers of music to have so many great musicians around and performing at the same time on stage, on radio, making recordings available on LPs, and even on television, which was becoming, slowly but surely, a key part of people's homes and lives. TV was earlier a part of radio, that is, a part of AIR services, but in the late '70s, TV became independent. TV brought the artiste, not just in voice, but also in look and presence, closer to a public that wanted this proximity. Doordarshan became increasingly proficient in programming. Music was always a big part of TV programmes. Remember *Chitrahaar*? Yes, it was revolutionary. Once a week, people watched it together and they made plans around it. People who did not own a TV would go to the homes of friends and neighbours to watch.

In the old days, royal courts and kings and the wealthy nobility supported the artiste. Now, times were different.

Courts and kings were already becoming a part of the past and they were not going to come back. This is the reason I believe that while our roots must be strong, we must be prepared to turn towards new directions as the world changes. Once upon a time, neither the singer nor the audience depended on technology. When technology came, it changed both. If you were heard and seen—in fact, the more you were heard and seen—the better were your chances of continually improving and enlarging your sphere of performance and influence.

Now all this was fine to a degree. It often raised the level of insecurity among some of the artistes. An unhappy and disappointing consequence of this was the build-up of jealousy and groupism. At some point, I began to sense a change in the atmosphere at music gatherings and studios. It happened very slowly and for a person like me, who in any case has no room for distraction where music is concerned, it took time before I became aware of this change. It seemed to be nothing initially. Small things. People talking about other people behind their backs. I never had room or reason to indulge in any of this. I did notice though, that it seemed as if the spirit of cooperation, collaboration and appreciation was diminishing. People seemed more focused on collecting small groups of supporters. It was a strange sort of competitiveness, where winning something rather than singing was becoming more important.

Gratitude be to Allah that my own teachers have never been like this, and that I was brought up to pay attention to my music, not to winning, losing or treating another artiste and musician as an opponent. Worse, to pretend to be an appreciative fellow artiste but to plan the downfall of the other! No. In my past, I have faced angry neighbours—but they were angry because my riyaz disturbed them. That was simple and straightforward. I could understand that!

I tried to keep away from all such groupism and concentrate on my music, but there came a time when the actions of others, some of whom were very respected and revered names in the field of music, started affecting me. Strange as it may seem to you, for the longest time, I just could not bring myself to believe that any of it was being done intentionally. Then one day, it was confirmed, to my utter disbelief and dismay, that there were singers who were actively trying to end my career. Therefore, it was not just about sabotaging a performance. Not just about a foolish act of pouring water on my head in front of an audience. It was about making sure that I was not invited to perform at any of the major concerts and sangeet sammelans. If you are not seen, not heard, the public is no longer a patron—you have no audience and nobody to support you.

I used to travel extensively around the country and abroad for my concerts in those days. I used to stay busy and out of local circulation due to these shows. As a result, some singers seized the chance to spread rumours among organizers of various music festivals in India that I had shifted abroad and was not interested in performing in India. Many times, I would have organizers tell me that they thought I would not be available or interested in performing at an event because 'someone' had told them that I had shifted base. When I asked them who was telling them these things, they would stay quiet. Their silence was enough for me to understand that these were big names in the field of music.

For example, I once performed at a prestigious music festival in Pune in 1977, where my performance was much appreciated and lauded by music lovers—yet, I never performed again at that festival. Later, I heard that there was another great singer who used his clout and all his influence to ensure that I never performed at that festival again. Such was his insecurity that he had told the organizers to tell the audience and my fans that the reason for my not being present there was because it was very difficult to contact me and that I had begun asking for a huge amount of money to perform. This was a lie. I decided to stay away from the situation because following up with any of the people concerned would have led to contentious interactions and conversations. This, I felt, would be demeaning to both—my music and me.

Therefore, I decided that I would deliberately hold on to the key aspects of who I am—an artiste, a musician, a singer, a composer, and sometimes a poet—the aspects that I valued. I would not entertain thoughts of countering the new trend of behaviour. Those things, I decided, were not my business. Allah has always found a way for my music and me, and I saw no reason for me to change that relationship of mine with the Almighty.

The years began to pass swiftly. I was in my forties and approaching half century. At this time, I found myself in the US. I had travelled there for a show and met a very old friend of mine. We were both happy to meet, and it had been many years—I think decades may have passed since we last met.

He wanted me to meet his son. After all, with the passage of time, all of us had reached the stage where our children and our families were at the core of our lives. Therefore, the next day, he drove me to his son's office, feeling quite excited, and I laughed at his pleasure and told him he was acting like a child. You can say these things to your dear friends and it does not matter that both are metaphorically ancient!

However, as we walked into the building, we both received a foretaste of what was going to happen, and it was uncomfortable. There was a receptionist in the lobby on the ground floor and she was as forbidding and disinterested in manner as we were excited. She asked us whom we had come to meet. My friend told her the name of his son. She nodded and asked him if he had an appointment with him.

Immediately, my friend replied, 'I'm his father. I've come to meet my son!'

'Yes,' said she, 'but do you have an appointment?'

I did not like this, but it was not my place to say anything. An appointment to meet your own children? I could not imagine a situation like this between me and Murtuza, who would have been at this time in his teens, or the little Rabbani, or any of the others—certainly not now and never in the years ahead. A small prayer went up from my heart to God for my children and their relationship with me.

Beginning to look both upset and embarrassed, my friend told her to simply inform his son that he was here. The receptionist looked at him with an expression that seemed terribly dismissive and disrespectful, but she did not repeat her question. She picked up the phone and left a message with someone at the other end.

I saw the look on my friend's face and I had to turn away because it hurt me. He looked deflated, and I saw that the pride and excitement we had walked in with was all gone. He was silent. We walked together to the chairs in the waiting area and sat down. I did not know what to say; small talk was unnecessary.

Five minutes later, his son came down and greeted both of us. He was very respectful and warm. He saw immediately that his father was upset and he asked him if something had happened. My friend could not help himself; he asked whether a father needs an appointment to meet his own son. Immediately, the young man apologized and then said the receptionist did not know, she was just doing her job. The matter ended there. We spent the next half hour together, but there was a little bit of strain. The excitement, the joy, it was gone.

My friend remained sad even as we drove back. I tried to make him feel better. I spoke of how different countries have different cultures and sometimes it takes strangers a little time to adjust. My friend responded then, saying that all over the world, there are parents and children and that relationship exists no matter the country or culture. It should not be hard to understand and give it the special space it deserves. I let him speak. I wanted him to feel better, and talking helps.

Silently, I told myself that I would not want my children to settle abroad or stay away from me. I would never let them forget our Hindustani culture and the interpersonal values that we have all been brought up with over generations.

It was also in 1980, that same year, that one day, I returned home at a time when Qadir would be doing his music riyaz with my father. Neither of them was aware that I was there, and I did not interrupt. As I listened to Qadir, my soul knew something—that this child, just eleven years old at the time, was ready for his next steps. If I was to keep my children connected to all that we are and all that I knew, I had to seize the day. I could not afford to miss milestones such as these. I immediately decided that henceforth, I would have him and Murtuza accompany me as often as possible on performance tours and for concerts. These are ways of opening doors for a child to step through and learn new things. These experiences become as important a part of learning as the technical nuances of your subject.

Experiencing life accompanied by your children is a wonderful thing. It brings you close and keeps you close as a family not by the mere fact of being physically present or travelling together, but because there are so many shared moments. On one occasion, after a show, I went with my sons to Aparna Sen's house for lunch. She was one of my students at the time. She was very fond of squirrels and had many in her house as pets. They were very comfortable with her and she with them—very much in the way you see people with their dogs or cats; they become like members of the family. We enjoyed our lunch very much. When we were returning home, my sons asked me who Aparna was speaking to in Bangla in her garden. I told them that she was speaking to her pet squirrels in Bangla, because that was the language they spoke at home. Not like some other squirrels who understood Marathi or the Rampur squirrels who understood Hindi. My sons looked seriously at me, I looked equally seriously at them, and then we all burst out laughing.

These are the little ways of looking at the world, experiencing it together. In these little ways, we achieve the strength of being together.

Children of the Seventies

Shahina

To me, my father has been the best father in the world. I realized this quite consciously, at an age when children become aware of other families and people around them. When I started comparing my father with other fathers around me, I was convinced that no other father was as caring as mine was. Yes, I remember being teased about this in school. A kind of 'my daddy best' competition began among friends and classmates. Everyone knew my father travelled a lot and was hardly home as much as the other fathers were, so I think that sometimes I defended his absence far more strongly than necessary.

Still, I think my daddy best. I laugh as I write this because even though I am laughing at myself just a little, I know this is what I truly feel.

I am the fifth child of my parents, born in 1973, so I am also the first of the '70s batch. This is important when you are in the middle, as I am, with four siblings always letting me know they are older than me, wiser than me, have known our parents longer than I have. So being the oldest of the '70s children was important to me growing up. I had my own younger ones to act older with!

I was a mischievous kid. I was a tree climber, a very good one. When I hear stories from Papa's childhood of his climbing lampposts, I feel the family should be proud of this agility that has been passed on to me. There were times when I would be comfortably sitting in a tree, feeling one with the leaves and the breeze and the sky, while the others would be looking for me around the house. At such times, Papa knew just where I would be! He would come looking for me and scold me, but somehow I knew, from the look in his eyes, that the scolding was for the sake of form. He felt it was his job to scold the daughter who climbed trees. So I never really stopped. Until I grew much older, of course, and then I lost interest. I did many naughty things when I was a child that sometimes got me, and sometimes my little brother Rabbani, into trouble. I did give my parents a difficult time, but I know they love me dearly. Sometimes, of course, things went too far and those times, I had to hide for a while. Such as the time I stole a plant from the neighbour's garden and put it in ours. The neighbour found out and instead of just coming over and being nice about it— after all, I was just a child—they wrote a letter to my father complaining to him about me. Oh, I knew I was in a lot of trouble when I heard my father call out to mom and ask her where I was! I had no option but to hide on the terrace for two hours so that he would not find me.

Then there was this other time, I must have been around six years old, when Papa brought a new radio from one of his trips abroad. My younger brother Rabbani and I got very excited upon seeing it and wanted to play it. We were asked not to touch it, much to our disappointment. So we were even more fascinated with it, this object we were not allowed to touch! On top of that, my oldest sister Nazma would play it as she pleased. She would turn it on and listen to it as she did her work or household chores. This, according to me, was not fair. I planned to do something about it, but I needed someone for moral support. Who would that be? Rabbani, of course! He has always been my partner in the plans I hatched. So I took him into confidence and told him we must explore this new thing, we must learn what it is about. I told him it was educational, that Papa and Mama would be happy to see us learning something new and being responsible with it.

One day, we got our chance and took the radio out to the terrace to investigate how it worked.

However, there was a problem.

Neither Rabbani nor I knew how to plug the thing into the electricity socket. I think I thought of us as two scientists inventing something new. We tried to plug it in, but got it horribly wrong. Rabbani, the baby—he was perhaps five at this time—must have been touching a wire or something because when I turned on the electric switch, the result was a big 'shock' for us.

The next thing I knew was that little Rabbani's hand, the one in which he was holding one end of the wire, was burnt. I saw, horrified, that his face had turned black. He was lying unconscious on the floor of the terrace. I panicked, ran downstairs and screamed for help so that someone would come and see what had happened to my little brother.

Everyone came rushing up. This was one of the rare times there was chaos in our house, because generally, our home was quite peaceful. Rabbani recovered quickly. He was bundled up in a blanket and put to bed. I think a neighbour or a doctor may have been called, but more than the electric shock, it was the shock of getting a shock that had knocked him out flat. I got a severe scolding that time. Rabbani was let off with a reprimand. Actually, this is the only time I recall Papa being very angry at what we had done. After his anger had abated, he called both of us and spoke to us calmly. He told us that he was not angry at our touching the radio, but was scared that since we were little children and did not know about the risks of playing with fire, electricity and water, we could have been very badly injured, or worse. We had to promise him that we would never do anything like that again. I was very scared at that time, and I have kept my promise to this day. Now I am middle-aged, but still careful how I touch a switch or an electrical gadget!

I wish I could say that is the last time I did anything naughty. No, I cannot say that. Here is another gem from my collection of stories. As Papa used to travel abroad quite extensively, we used to have some foreign currency lying at home. Besides the paper currency, there was a sizeable collection of coins from various countries, which fascinated me. I found the shiny gold and silver coins intensely alluring and loved playing with them.

I was just about twelve when I once went with Papa and saw him exchanging some foreign currency and coins for Indian currency. This gave me an idea. I thought brightly to myself that if Papa could do it, I could do it too, to enhance my pocket money. So one day, I took Rabbani with me to the same shop to exchange some currency and coins that I had picked up from somewhere around the house, to exchange it all at the money changer's office. Rabbani, my staunch and loyal supporter, looked quite excited with the whole adventure. I always liked this in him. He did not try to talk me out of things. He would let me talk him into things.

I think the person at the currency exchange office recognized me. He told us to wait, then went across to the neighbouring shop and called up Papa. He told him that I was there with my brother to exchange some foreign coins.

Meanwhile, Rabbani and I waited with some excitement for our efforts to bear fruit. Imagine our feelings then, when a few minutes later, we heard Papa's voice behind us. We turned around and saw him standing there, looking quite angry. I think that if I could have, I would have run away and hid as I did when I had stolen the neighbour's plant! However, Papa was standing in front of the only entry and exit. He took us away from there and on the way home, scolded us for what we had done. Do you know what he said? He warned us that if we did something like that again, the police might arrest us and put us in jail. In jail? I was twelve. Rabbani was eleven. Our hearts almost stopped beating. I am sure my face went white with fear. At some point, I recall that Papa looked at me and stopped his scolding mid-sentence. Then he tapped me on the head and told me that this was another sort of thing I was never to do again. He was very sure it was my idea. He knew me and he knew Rabbani. I think I was close to tears; I may even have shed some. As swiftly as his anger had spilled out into the scolding, it vanished. He shook his head at me and then told us both he felt like an ice cream. Would we also like some?

Would we? I must tell you no ice cream ever tasted better.

This is my father. The best in the whole world. He had long hair, so I loved making ponytails for him, and he would let me! Whenever Mom scolded me, he would try to save me. When I was scared at night, I would go and wake him up so that he would ask me to sleep next to Mom and him. When I was tired at night after playing all day, and crying, complaining of body aches, he would press my arms and legs with his hands. The days he came home tired, I would make him tea and massage his head. These were a part of life and all our relationships at home. I believe he consciously created this environment with Mom for all of us. We would have considered it extremely unusual if any of us were cold or uncaring of anyone within the family, among ourselves, or of other people. These are ways of being that nobody teaches you in a book or in school—you either live them or you do not. We did.

Papa used to give me pocket money, and tell me to hide it from Mom because she would try to make me save it! Sometimes when going out, he would ask for change, and I would give him the 10-20 paise that I did actually save from my pocket money. He would take it, kiss the coins, touch them to his forehead and keep them in his pocket. It is possible that I saved them for him, just because I loved that he did this.

I was so mischievous that he would scold me saying '*Har waqt sirf shaitaani hi karti rehti ho, mujhe tumhare hath ki roti khani hai* (You are naughty all the time. I want to eat rotis made by you).' Actually, that is how I learnt to cook—all because of him. He was very encouraging, he would tell me, '*Tum jaisi bhi roti banaogi mai khaunga* (I will eat whatever kind of roti you make).' So I would make rotis. I found it to be great fun. It was a little bit like playing. You could make shapes, but you could not control the shape as you rolled it out. At least, I could not. Then when I cooked them, I sometimes burnt them. If my mother saw them, she would get irritated. However, my father? Oh, he ate them all. I started loving cooking because of him.

Teenage is a difficult period. I know that with each of us, when we were teenagers, he would spend extra time talking, explaining things, listening to us talk about what was happening in school and in our heads at the time. Because he has always made sure he remained close to us, we were able to speak to him quite unselfconsciously about many things. He got us through our teens with a lot of love and understanding. I have heard many people say that you lose touch with your children once they hit their teens. Never was this true in our family. See, it was not that we talked all the time about everything, no. However, we remained close and we remained caring of each other. That came through for us; it held us together and kept us happy.

When I grew up, I became friends with all of his students, whom he would treat like his own kids.

Then, one day, my marriage was fixed. I was very excited about all the clothes and wedding arrangements, so he asked me to wear all my outfits, along with the shoes, and show him how I looked. I did. He looked at me with tears in his eyes and said, '*Acchi lag rahi ho* (you are looking good).' That is when I realized that marriage would mean I was going to go away from this home, this family and the best father in the whole world, to live elsewhere, with other people. My tree-climbing, coin-pocketing days were over. As a kid, I always believed I would never leave my father's house. The day I got married, I hugged Papa and cried a lot. After I left, for a while, he would call me every day, and unbelievably, we would both cry.

All of us are very attached to Papa and it has always been this way. Mom would often complain that we loved him more than her.

He is a legendary musician to the world, but with his kids, he is the best father you can ever imagine. He gave us as much of his love and time as he could and went out of his way to keep us happy.

* * *

Rabbani

My father once said to me, '*Tumko dekhta hun, toh mujhe apni jawani yaad aati hai* (Whenever I see you, I am reminded of my youth).' He seemed to refer to the passion and single-minded focus I bring to my work. I am a film producer and singer by profession. I think that is one of the best compliments I have ever received, especially as it came from my dear father, who is the pride of my life. Everyone says I look and sound more like my father than any of my siblings—that quality described as voice texture. Mine is closest to my father's.

I was born in 1974. The '70s were a time when Papa had a hectic schedule of travel and performances, within the country and abroad. I am told that when I was very young and I knew that Papa was about to leave the house, I would cry and assume it was going to be many days before he returned. Even if he was just going around the corner for some work, I would make a big fuss, wail and not let him leave the house. This is what I have been told and I have to say, I think it is quite possible I really was like this! Anyway, if he could take me with him—suppose he was just going for a bit of work or chores close by—he would. However, if he were leaving on a performance tour, he made sure that either I was sleeping at the time he exited the house, or he would actually put me to bed and ensure that I was asleep before he left. Perhaps I woke up and wailed when I found he was not in the house, but I cannot remember that either. The others say I did.

I do recall a time when I was perhaps five years old and was seeing Papa after a long time. He had just returned from a show abroad. I wanted to spend some time with him and asked him whether I could miss school the next day, half expecting him to refuse immediately. He was very strict about his children going to school and getting taaleem. He surprised me. I could not believe it when he smiled and told me I could, but only on one condition, that I get up early, get dressed and make my bed at the usual time the next day. I was delighted. I slept with the thought of a day out of school spent with my father. I made plans. We could go out, buy some snacks, and maybe a new toy or game would be mine before the day ended! The others would certainly be at school, which meant that I would have my father all to myself! Therefore, I woke up the next day, got ready, made the bed and went off to tell him I was done.

He smiled at me with a twinkle in his eye and said, 'That's my good boy.' Then he said, 'Now that you have gotten ready and been a good boy, why don't you become an even better boy by going to school? There's a good half an hour still, so you will reach on time.'

I stared at him. I could not believe my ears and blurted out, 'B . . . but you said . . .'

He ruffled my hair, laughed and asked me to look at the calendar on the wall.

I did. The date was 1 April.

I looked back at Papa and gathered all my breath, getting ready to wail out my disappointment, but he shook his head and looked at me with so much love that I just had to accept I had been pranked! It was April Fools' Day. I was not going to skip school. There was nothing more to say, so I reluctantly picked up my school bag and left for school. He made sure, though, that I did not feel bad or let down by this. When school got over and we were home free, he took us out that day. I remember we went to the local market and had a lot of fun choosing a few things we wanted for ourselves. I do not remember the things, but I remember being together.

This is what made childhood special for us all. We got things, we had fun, we were disciplined, we could not miss school or riyaz, we had to learn to be polite and respectful of each other and of others too, but most importantly, we had these relationships. The bond with our parents was strong. My mother was the one who ensured that our daily care and routine continued without interruption and that we stayed out of trouble. My father ensured that he always stayed connected and close to us. The way we grew up, we learnt to look out for each other, stand up for each other, do things together and value the relationships we had, and have, with each other.

To be the son of a man so loved and appreciated all over the world is an amazing experience. It is like no other. He is my father, but he shines no less for me than he does for any of his fans and supporters. We must remain grounded. It is easy to bask in the admiration and esteem people hold him in, it is easy to think of ourselves as an extension of this person, therefore deserving of the same. This is, of course, not true. Not only would he never allow us to think or behave in this way, he also instilled in us the ambition to earn our own achievements and make our own path. He inspired us. I do not mean that we went separate ways, ever; I mean that he ensured that we had the freedom of spirit to shape our own personalities and individuality. This was not easy because in the life that we shared with him, especially when we brothers began to accompany him for performances, we lived with the spotlight shining brightly on us as well.

I remember, once when I was grown up and accompanying him along with my older brothers to performances, we were in Paris. We were travelling in two cars, moving towards the venue, which was ten minutes away on foot, but it took more than an hour by car due to heavy traffic. As we reached the venue, we realized that the tanpura was not with us in the car, but had been left behind in the hotel room. So we brothers swiftly walked back to the room, got the tanpura and managed to reach the venue in time for the show. That was when I realized that the show was sold out, and there were some people gatecrashing and lots of pandemonium. It was becoming difficult for the organizers to handle the crowd. We, meanwhile, were quietly slipping in through an entrance for performers and staff when suddenly, a stranger, a local man from Paris who desperately wanted to get in, requested us to give him the tanpura to him and let him walk in with us! Such was the passion for Papa's music. In our own country, the craze for classical music is not so great.

Sometimes I think about these things and I feel we need to bring back a sense of valuing what we take for granted—our music, our artistic and cultural traditions, our heritage. We need to expand the audience circle and devise creative ways by which we can introduce our own Hindustani classical music to more people, across age and social groups. This I love about my father—he has always been open to doing new things with new people, reaching out to different audiences, experimenting with sounds and styles. In 2013, we did a three-generation performance with A.R. Rahman for Coke Studio, in which my father, my brothers Murtuza, Qadir and Hasan, Faiz, who is Murtuza's son, and I, all took the stage together for an incredibly rewarding performance. Audiences across India and the world have loved it. This is what we have learnt and received from my father—to open the doors to new possibilities, to keep learning and doing new things even as we cherish and protect the old traditions.

* * *

Hasan

I have always called my Papa 'Tan Mian' because I would always see him singing *tans*. When you are the youngest, actually the second youngest, of the children in a family like ours, the path is set out for you in many ways, not just by parents but also by the older siblings. I am the seventh of eight brothers and sisters. There is but one younger than I, Rabia, my kid sister. She is not a kid anymore, of course, none of us are kids anymore, but those who have siblings know that through life, you see each other the way you did growing up. So you think of the older ones as older and the younger ones as kids forever!

By the time I was old enough to be conscious of the particular and unique routines of a family steeped in classical music traditions, I had already become familiar with song, voice and riyaz. My father and my brothers followed a practice schedule, even if my father was not home all the time. Our grandfather taught my brothers and would oversee riyaz routines. I think that in the beginning, when I was very little, I may have actually believed that this is how everyone lived in his or her home, that the practice of music was a part of life. As I started growing up, I realized that it was my father's life's work and a very difficult path to follow.

It is the way of a close-knit family like ours to introduce even the youngest, such as I was, into the artistic life early. Just listen, Papa would tell me when I was old enough to respond and focus for short periods. Just listen and you will learn, he would say. That is how I began my life and my musical journey. My father is my ustad, my teacher, and now, I work with him as I train his students alongside him. These artistic traditions would slip away if they were not kept alive by the passion and dedication of a few. My exposure to the world of music, performances, classical traditions and audiences is because of all these members of my family and I am grateful to have been so blessed.

* * *

Rabia

Born in 1977, I am the youngest and perhaps the most pampered of all my brothers and sisters. There are so many advantages of being the youngest that the disadvantages fade! For example, while I have sometimes seen Papa get upset with one of the others for doing something dangerous or terribly foolish, I have never seen him upset with me. In fact, I may even go so far as to say that Papa has never shouted at any of his children and has always been a very calm and understanding father.

I have spent many minutes, which could add up to days, on my father's back pretending that he is a *ghoda* (horse) and I am a horse rider. Yes! Ustad Ghulam Mustafa Khan, my father, used to keep me entertained and happy as a child by trotting about the house, and sometimes pretending to collapse because he would say the rider was too heavy!

As I was growing up, the one thing I felt most steadily was the way he loved and cared for each of us. He knew who our particular friends were at any point of our lives, he knew our interests and he knew if something was bothering one of us. His absence due to his travel schedule never translated into absence as a father. I have learnt so many things from just experiencing life at home. For example, my father's warmth and hospitality is legendary. People would come home at odd hours, but Papa would always want them to eat and be comfortable. Once, we had a guest who dropped in past midnight. We had all finished dinner. There was very little left over. My mother told Papa that she was worried as the fridge just had a little leftover rice and some mutton in a bit of gravy. Papa told her to convert it into a biryani style dish, mixing the gravy into the rice and adding the mutton. You will not believe it, but the guest was overwhelmed by being served a meal so flavourful, and at that time of the night! I always think of this story as Papa's instant biryani recipe, but the reason it is special to me is the spirit behind it. We made sure that no guest ever left without feeling the affection, attention and warmth of home!

Papa has always enjoyed a good home-cooked meal, but his favourite foods are dry preparations, with tandoori chicken on top of the list. He also likes manchow soup very much. His real fondness, though, is for sweets. He just cannot resist them. Zarda is his favourite sweet and whenever he is at home, he demands it! Even now, his love for sweets remains. We tell him to be careful and not eat them for his well-being, and so he pretends that he is not interested, but I have caught him eating something sweet on the quiet many times!

Do you remember that old ad on TV, for a bulb? The jingle was '*Jab main chhota bachcha tha, badi shararat karta tha. Meri chori pakdi jaati* (I was very naughty as a child; my little thefts would be caught) . . .' Well, exactly the same thing happened to Papa and me once. I was about fourteen and I caught Papa eating sweets from the fridge at two o'clock in the night! I was too young to say anything to him, so I started singing the jingle and we both burst out laughing. I kept his secret, but he too did not eat any more sweets that night.

Papa is an unusual human being. You would imagine, if you did not know him, that he would be aloof, distant, would keep himself apart from everyone in a dignified way. He is not like this. Full of great spirit and energy, he embodies the phrase 'young at heart'. There was this time he had just returned from one of his programmes and was entering the building when the neighbourhood kids told him that their ball had gone over to the other side of the wall and they were unable to fetch it. Papa promptly jumped across the boundary ball and retrieved the ball for them. Up until a few years ago, he was climbing guava trees to pluck the fruit for my son!

Ustad Ghulam Mustafa Khan, music maestro, but also the best father and grandfather anyone could ever wish for!

When my youngest sister-in-law, Rabia Awadh, the youngest child of Ustad Ghulam Mustafa Khan, sat down with me to tell me her stories, I noticed another factor common to all the stories from each of his children, now adults—that he has always been, and still is, a person of an uncomplicated, down-to-earth and simple nature.

I have seen his gentleness with people, his own family and others, play a part in every conversation and interaction, be it ever so mundane or of great significance. Take this matter of cooking, for example. At least two of his daughters have specifically mentioned how they learnt how to cook and began to enjoy cooking because he would eat whatever they made, even the most terrifying of their childhood experiments. In some way, he translated an approach to teaching and learning across subjects. For him, the importance of riyaz, practice, in his own life and in the lives of his students, comes from an understanding that making mistakes and achieving expertise are at opposite ends of doing. You must first do something, only then can a mistake happen. Even the most practised expert can slip sometimes, and hence the importance of continuing to practise. Gentleness has been his way of life, his way of interacting with other human beings. My mom-in-law has experienced this too. He was always very appreciative of her cooking and the few times when, inadvertently, something was not cooked the way it should have been, he made sure he never said anything to hurt her feelings.

Rabia tells me another story. When her father would do his riyaz late into the night, he would put his mouth inside a glass so that the sound was muffled and the children would not be disturbed. In my mind, I can see him when he was a young man, still in his teens, living alone in Lucknow amid strangers who did not appreciate a musician who practiced singing in the silence and peace of the night. This person cleaned out a filthy room in the back of a house and continued nightly riyaz with his head in a matka to muffle the sound. There is a continuity to his dedication and to his ability to find a solution for others, even if it means putting himself in more than a little discomfort.

Rabia says that when the children would ask him why he practised so much, he would smile and tell them that he was learning something new every day from his performances, from his experiences and from his riyaz. Somehow, then, learning was never associated with being a child in the house. Everyone valued learning or the attempt another person was making to learn something. Nobody laughed at someone who made a mistake or did not know how to do something. I have grown up seeing such high value placed on effort and persistence that these were actually held to be more important than the achievement that emerged as a result. These are the lessons we learnt; they never get old or outdated.

Forever young, forever learning. Ustad Ghulam Mustafa Khan.

Music and singing run in the family. Sometimes, a framework of family history and social culture looks at sons as the followers of their father. Daughters may appear to be less focused upon, particularly when the art and occupation being discussed is music and singing. Historically, for women to go out in public and perform at shows and events has always been a big challenge. Traditionally, when fathers and ancestors are the source of a practice and of learning, it often happens that the mantle of carrying on the traditional knowledge is worn in the same way across generations. Some family traditions continue through the sons, some through the eldest son alone. Daughters alone may carry other traditions forward. Mostly the sons, with each successive generation, have carried the musical traditions of this family forward.

This does not mean that the women and daughters of the family are disconnected from music traditions. In our family, Papa's own mother played a key role in his training as a child. She herself came from a family with a great music tradition and she understood and appreciated both the discipline within the tradition as well as the practice of it. Then there is Ammi, also from a family with a rich history of classical music. She knew from day one, she never needed an explanation, of the sort of home environment that she would be a part of, that she would need to create, to sustain both the music and the artiste. As Papa often says, were it not for her, the kind of person that she is, he would not have had the freedom and peace of mind to achieve much of what he has. At family functions, women do gather together to sing traditional songs, and they enjoy these private gatherings a great deal. They just have not chosen singing as a career.

For some people who find themselves caught between the ways of the old days, and the contemporary world of shifting perspectives on these things, it is hard to understand that many of the individuals, women and men, in these relationships are content with the ways of some of these particular traditions. Therefore, yes, people close to the family, who visited them at home, often said things like 'aapki bachchiyan bhi sur main gaati hain (Even your daughters sing tunefully and well).'

In the stories Papa has shared, the 1990s as a decade, have a completely different quality to them. The children are adults. There are marriages and marriage arrangements. There are shows and concerts that are now performed as a family of musicians. As life progresses, the parent continues to shine through, whether a city is riot-torn, or money is needed for wedding preparations, or grown-up sons are craving curry in a foreign land. These events do not all hold the same sense of urgency or level of anxiety, but they all have importance in the heart of a man who has seen life span many things—good, bad, funny—and given it all its due.

My Elder Brother, My Ustad

Aftab Ahmed Khan

I started learning music from my father, Ustad Waris Hussain Khan sahib, and then later, my eldest brother, Ustad Ghulam Mustafa Khan, continued my training. He taught me everything about raags and symphonies. When he would practise in the night, he would call me and ask me to sit next to him. He wanted me to have the chance to listen, as he has always said that in listening, there is great learning, so that I could pick up the intricacies of classical music. One of my earliest memories is of watching my elder brother practise his music and sing through the night. I have understood from watching him that the only way to get something right is to repeat it until you get it right. Then to repeat it yet again, so that it stays right. That if you make a mistake, you must start over. Do not ignore the mistake, it will not correct itself. There is a hard self-discipline at the core of riyaz, as I have learnt from him. There is also a great deal of honesty in riyaz when you are alone. When you practise by yourself and there is nobody around to listen or to witness your stumbles and your weaknesses, it is entirely up to you to make the effort and correct yourself. It may seem to an untrained listener or audience member that a performer has a natural gift and talent, that the performance comes easy to the performer, but to my knowledge, this is rarely, if ever, true. Creativity, performance and art—they bring pleasure to the audience and to the individual pursuing them, but this pleasure always comes with steadfastness and the ability to persist. I learnt these things along with music, because I saw these qualities in my brother.

I would sit during his riyaz until about 1 a.m. This is when he would ask me to go and sleep. I did not sleep, though I would leave so he could continue peacefully. I used to hide behind a pillar and watch him do his riyaz until early morning. Of course, he never got to know this. I would be silent, I would not even sneeze. This way, I learnt more than he thought I was learning, and later, surprise him by singing the same raag for him the next day. Now that I listen to myself telling you this story, I realize he must have known what I was up to! However, being the ustad that he is, he let me do as I did because I so actively and consciously learnt so much more, with even greater focus, in this way.

His temperament is such that even when he is annoyed or is in a bad mood, he never gets angry with another. Still, it has always bothered me whenever I have found him in a bad mood, because he does not let us know what is upsetting him until much later. I make light of things then, crack jokes, try to get his mood to change, and then I ask him what has upset him. I remember, our father used to smoke, but bhai sahib is allergic to smoke and gets a cough if somebody is smoking around him. When father would smoke, bhai sahib would be annoyed but, out of respect and courtesy, would never say anything. He would silently walk out of the room. When he did that, father would understand and crushing his beedi, would get him back into the room.

Family has always meant a lot to bhai sahib. He brought us up, taught us music and when our mother passed away, became even more consciously responsible and available to us. He loved all his three sisters and they were very fond and supportive of him.

During the rains, his favourite season of the year, he would avoid travelling abroad. That was one thing that could distract him from music, if there ever was anything. Rains to him meant family and hot pakoras.

I am happy to say I have done many shows with him and some of them are memorable for reasons other than music. He will never let me forget how, at a performance in Akola, I took away the mic from in front of him because mine had suddenly stopped working. I did it unthinkingly and because I am so used to him; he is my brother, I have known him from my infancy. It just came naturally to me. It is a story he loves, and we have all heard it many times.

Once, I remember, we had a show in Gwalior on 23 December, and it was freezing cold. Bhai sahib had a fever, but he performed on stage till 2 a.m., and not once did he let the audience feel that he was feeling cold or unwell. Such was his commitment and dedication to his music and his audience.

I have watched bhai sahib grow into a musician of enormous influence, appreciated by listeners in different parts of the world. I remember that in the decade of the '70s, he did many shows in Afghanistan. Ustad Mohammad Hussain Sarahanga, a famous and beloved musician in Afghanistan, who himself came from a family with strong musical traditions, had studied music in India. He had many fans in India as well. He heard bhai sahib perform and loved it so much that he began to organize concerts for him in Afghanistan. He would attend each one of these. Unfortunately, he passed away soon after, in the early 1980s.

When I think of my brother, I am always struck by the way he is loved and his music appreciated by people from all over the world. Bhai sahib always underplays this. He says it is the music that touches and connects with people and that is what they love. I think he does not always realize that it is also him, his personality and the way he comes across to people, that is an important part of the magic of his music.

My One-of-a-kind Mamu Sahib

Ustad Rashid Khan

Ustad Ghulam Mustafa Khan sahib is my maternal uncle and I consider him to be like a father. It is amazing to see that his enthusiasm and dedication towards music is the same as it was when he was young. It is a delight to watch him sing with as much practice, riyaz and preparedness as he did earlier.

There was a time when only the Agra gharana and the Patiala gharana were known in the field of Hindustani classical music. I am proud of the fact that, with his excellence and dedication, he has made a name for the Rampur gharana and brought it into limelight and at par with the other famous music gharanas.

The most amazing thing about him is that he still has the same drive and stubbornness to do something special in music and to keep honing his art.

Ustad Ghulam Mustafa Khan is one of a kind and I can say with certainty that people like him are not born every day.

In the 1980s, Papa did some beautiful music for Muzaffar Ali's film Umrao Jaan. He did three unforgettable songs, of which Raagmala is outstanding in its dramatic time progression, building the life of Rekha's character in the film. People still talk about this, discussing the raags that were sequenced and the way they were so perfectly put together into a whole composition. For the rest of us, for his students and his audience, it is easy to understand how someone can become so ardent a fan of Ustad Ghulam Mustafa Khan.

Despite having lent his voice to the music of films, Papa is not much of a film viewer and in fact, has probably seen not more than three films, if that many, in his entire life. I have never seen him take time out for himself. He has taken time out for his children, yes. However, I do not believe he would consider the two or three hours it takes to sit through a film to be hours he is willing to give up thus.

People from other countries, other cultures, have communicated with him and asked him if he would be their teacher. He has had many foreign students who have wanted to learn classical music from him. Usually, they have all been very aware of the traditions and etiquette of a Hindustani classical music class, including the appropriate attire.

As the classes are held sitting on the floor, it is necessary for students to be attired so that it is easy for them to sit cross-legged. One of the stories I have heard is about a girl student who was not aware of this; she wore clothes that were not appropriate. You know how difficult it is to sit on the floor wearing a tight, short dress or a mini skirt. Obviously, even though this student was completely comfortable in these outfits, she found it difficult to sit on the floor. Despite this, she continued to wear her customary short dresses, not realizing that besides causing her trouble, they were also causing embarrassment to the other students and to Papa.

When, after even three or four classes, the girl did not realize that she should wear something more suited to the class, Papa gently but firmly told her that if she wanted to learn Indian classical music, she must also dress like an Indian. The important thing here is that he spoke to her without causing her any embarrassment, in a way that the others did not hear what was said.

The student understood what Papa meant and from the next day, her attire was different; sitting on the floor caused nobody any embarrassment, including her.

Just as sometimes, a different culture and way of life can lead to a funny or difficult situation, not being proficient in a language can do the same. You could be praising someone, and they could be thinking that you are using bad language! In this next story, Papa was praising another person in Urdu.

Lauding the person on his achievements, Papa told him, 'Allah ne apne alava tumhe sab se bekhauf kar diya hai (Besides Himself, God has made you fearless of everyone else).'

The person did not understand the meaning of the word 'bekhauf', and in fact, he thought Papa had said 'bewakoof'. Bekhauf means fearless. Bewakoof means foolish.

Though he did not say anything to Papa, he was quite offended by his comment and wondered why Papa had called him foolish!

It was only later, when he happened to mention this exchange to my brother-in law, Murtuza, that Bhai told him the correct meaning of the word. This is when he finally understood that Papa was not calling him a fool.

He promptly apologized for thinking so and everyone had a good laugh, including Papa, who heard the story later.

The tales ahead include some less funny episodes involving infatuated fans. Hard as it is to believe, infatuation can become a threat to life and home, and Papa and the rest of the family certainly have experienced these situations at various times!

When the Cold Weather Leads to Composition and Other Stories

I travelled to Canada in 1984. It was an unusually cold year and it was freezing up there. I was now no longer a young man, having crossed the half century mark a few years ago! I have always had to be careful about ear, nose and throat problems. Ordinarily irritating for all, they spell disaster to a singer.

Fortunately, I was staying with a friend who had central heating in his house. I was quite comfortable and getting used to the warmth inside as opposed to the cold outside, but then, the constant heat from the central heating got to me. All of a sudden, I felt suffocated. I told my friend how I was feeling and I quickly went up to the top floor, opened a window and put my head outside. The cold breeze hit my face and I started feeling good.

Suddenly, my friend, who had followed me upstairs, worried, came up behind me and scolded me, 'What are you doing? You will fall ill!'

I laughed at the anxious expression on his face and told him, 'I can't sit inside this closed, centrally heated room. It's very comfortable, but it is not for me!'

Soon, I was feeling better. I sent my friend off to sleep and told him I would stay up a while longer before I went to bed. Amazingly, in that strange cold weather, occasionally still sticking my head out of the window, a bandish came to me in Pahadi Thumri . . . *'Baaton baaton main beet gayi raat, sajan tum rooth gaye.'*

I chuckled to myself. This was a new experience. A cold night in Canada and a bandish! I could not help myself. I woke up my friend from his deep sleep and asked him for his tape recorder to quickly record this composition before it escaped from my mind. Friends understand each other. My friends understand that the creative impulse is a reality. It can strike you anywhere, at any time. If you ignore it then, if you disrespect it, you risk losing something special. So that is how we spent a cold night in a room with the window open a crack, the freezing cold breeze finding its way in through that crack, recording my bandish.

There is something about the gift we call creativity that does not always do well when mixed with commercial intention. I can speak only for myself, not for anyone else. Being immersed in music is all the reward I have sought from music. Yes, I understood at a very young age how important it is to be practical, to have the money for the things you or your family need. Still, it is not a simple matter of buying and selling when it comes to my music. Not at all. Music and money do not walk together. When I am invited to sing, to perform before an audience, to do a recording, my first thought is never about what will I be paid. Sometimes, it is not a thought at all. I think, dream and plan the performance. What should I sing? What will the audience connect with?

Which sequence should I plan? What is appropriate for the occasion?

I stay away from the commercialization of life and art. Let those for whom commerce is important pursue it or be guided by it. It is not for me. It irks me, these conversations about money that I sometimes overhear or that people sometimes try to have with me. Who was paid how much, who charges how much for a show, what is the going rate. How does all this matter? I do not have time or interest in all this. Music is not potatoes and onions. I do not sing better, and I do not sing more, if you pay me more. I do not sing badly, or one song less than my plan, if you pay me less. What is more? What is less? Who decides the price of song? It is about hits, I have heard people say. Hits? I find this very strange. A song becomes a hit, you hear it everywhere one day, and it is nowhere two days later because there is a new hit. Then, my children explained the internet to me. Or at least, they tried to explain it—how many times people have heard you and seen you. But none of this has anything to do with why you sing, how you sing, how you compose and create music. Or create anything. Leave all this talk of money and music aside. I am not interested.

Therefore, here is a story I remember of my first performance in Pakistan. I was quite popular in Pakistan, but despite repeated invitations from there, I always said that I would come to Pakistan only under the aegis of the Indian high commission. Finally in 1987, I was cleared by our High Commission to perform in Karachi and Islamabad, at the invitation of a famous and popular Pakistani artiste, Tufail Niazi. He enjoyed my music greatly. He was also a good friend of mine and loved me like a brother. What happened there was that because I had refused to discuss the financials with the organizers beforehand, the remuneration they offered me was what may be described as neither appropriate nor fair to an artiste. Tufail got very upset with the Pakistani authorities and organizers for not paying what he knew was just and correct. I told him that I'd actually never really cared for all that. That for me, my music was everything and I was satisfied and happy to reach out to as many people as I could. Tufail would have none of it and in front of me, he told his people that by not paying what I deserved to be paid, they had insulted a great musician. I was quite overwhelmed at his support and love for me, but told him gently that I had not come to Pakistan to perform for money but for his friendship and love.

It was also important to me that Qadir, my son, who had accompanied me to Pakistan, learns how to deal with such situations with dignity and self-respect. It was his first experience of a performance outside the country. I am glad he was with me and observed some of these interactions. Many of them took place in his presence.

During my long journey as a classical musician, I have known and been aware of many who have loved and appreciated my music. You call them 'fans'. Therefore, there have been enthusiastic fans, both male and female, in India and abroad. I have received a great deal of adulation and respect and overall, my relationship with my fans has been one of love and affection. I would say that the love and respect has been mainly for my craft rather than me as a person. I think that to be a fan, a person must also be very familiar with the subject of their passion. To be able to appreciate another's work with such intense feelings and loyalty is to give a gift. To be appreciated to such a degree can be a strange experience—one must be very practical and grounded to do so. Just as artistes are not a faceless group of people, fans aren't either. Each artiste has an individual identity, a personality. So does every fan. In that crowd of people clapping and shouting, not one person is exactly like another. This is important to understand. I think humility is one of the most important aspects of one's relationship with fans.

However, there have been instances in which a fan has crossed the line and behaved badly. They failed to separate the man from the music. This has led to some embarrassing and some decidedly strange experiences for me.

There was this one instance when I was abroad, where this young girl was so enamoured that she fell in love with me. She wanted to possess me, and I don't think it mattered to her that I was already a married man with children and that I had no interest in pursuing any kind of relationship except that of a teacher and a guru with my fans. Unfortunately, this girl was so far removed from reality that her adulation for me became an obsession. She would write letters, she would try to meet me, she would leap out at me unexpectedly in different places; I think she used to follow me. I did not at any point let her feel I was at all interested in any of this. I felt deeply disturbed by her behaviour. I wanted her to stop accosting me. I wanted her to understand that she had built up some big picture in her head about herself and me and it was not real, and I was not interested. I had to tell performance organizers and those who accompanied me to be aware that she could create a disturbance at any time. Those people then spoke to her to try to make her understand that she needed to stop behaving like this.

When she realized that there was no way she could have a relationship with me, she decided that if I could not be hers, she would make sure that I did not have any relationship with anyone else either. Those around me told me that she had openly threatened to poison me. For a while, everyone got very worried and made sure I was never alone. This was becoming a little irritating. Then, as suddenly as she had stormed into my circle, she dropped out of it. Well, I am alive today, so I guess better sense must have prevailed, or perhaps her friends and family persuaded her to return to reality.

Another instance that caused me discomfort was when a female disciple of mine, herself a very well-known singer, believed she was in love with me. Like all my other disciples, she too used to come to my house to learn music from me and I never knew when she developed such a fondness for me. It only started becoming apparent when she would call up at odd hours to speak to me and talk about things that were not really related to music. She knew I was a married man with children, but she still sought a relationship with me. I stopped taking her calls. Amina was very upset with this situation. She spoke to me about it and said that before the whole thing got out of hand and became an embarrassment for everybody, it should be nipped right in the bud. She said that when someone crosses a line such as this, then it means they do not respect other people and their lives. She felt that this girl should no longer train under me, certainly not come over to our house for lessons, nor call up or have anything to do with me. Therefore, the story of this infatuation ended there.

I think perhaps that sometimes, there are some people who have not yet found their own anchor, the one within. We do not know many things about the life of another person. I believe, for myself, that it is important to understand intent— first your own, and then somebody else's. Sometimes, when a person who loves my music showers me with their adoration, I am clear that my intent around that person is to enjoy their appreciation of my music, not to let them think that I am interested in a personal involvement outside of my life with my family. It becomes important to identify your own seat of pride and ego. It feels nice to be adored, but at what cost and to what end?

Through Cities, Concerts and Children Growing Up

In 1992, Qadir, my son, started performing solo all over India. I was proud of him and very happy. He would call me before every performance and say, 'Papa, *mere liye dua kariyega* (Please pray for me).' I remember that I too would call him every day, and one of the things I always told him is that I missed him. Your children need to know that you love them and you are thinking of them, no matter how grown up they are. Later, as I recall, he gave his first international performance in Hong Kong. I knew that he was well on his way along his own musical path. I would tell him, '*Mehnat kar rahe ho, fateh karoge* (You are working hard, you will conquer).'

Of the '90s, I remember the year 1993 very well. If I think of events at the beginning of the decade, that is the year I jump to. There are many reasons for this. Shadma, who had been doing her BEd, got married that year after completing the course. The year began with tension in Bombay due to the riots that spilled over into January from the December of 1992. I remained in Bombay through January to be with my family. Amina and I wanted to maintain normalcy in our home as far as possible. We used to take Shadma in a taxi, sitting between us, to attend her B.Ed. classes. As the year progressed, the situation improved. As things calmed down, the city returned to normal and people to their routines. So did I. This meant travelling again for music performances.

Now I had entered my seventh decade and rather than slowing down, as many people seem to feel they ought to when they hit sixty, I found this to be my busiest time. I was singing at shows all over the country and had no time to either visit home or devote any time to my family. On top of that, Shadma's wedding date had been fixed. I was literally at my wits' end. I did not know how my wife would be able to manage all the preparations in my absence and without any help from me. I knew that she was a highly capable and resourceful person, but I felt guilty about not being able to be there when I was needed most. At about this time, I had a commitment for a concert in Delhi, for the Kwality and Gaylord people. They were considered the first family of restaurateurs at the time. The show was attended by the most high-profile section of Delhi's social circle and was greatly appreciated by them.

My next performance was in Allahabad. At that time, flights were not available for all sectors, so one had to travel by train. Amina was not happy that I could not return, but she quickly recovered and worked out a solution for her own requirements. Wedding preparations require money. She told me I would need to get money across to her, even if it meant I had to break my journey somewhere. I looked at the train schedule and realized Rampur was a good stop for us to coordinate, so I told her to meet me there. When my train reached Rampur, there she was at the station. I jumped off, handed her the money, much to her relief and delight, and carried on by the same train to Allahabad. Today, when I recall and tell you this story, I think of what strange times we have lived through—meeting my wife at a train station between concert commitments to hand over money for our daughter's wedding preparations. Preparations that I simply could not be a part of, no matter how much I wanted to be there. It was an emotional journey for me. This little girl, whom I had fed with my own hands when she was little, whom I would follow to school to make sure she was safe, the child who loved the Makhdoom Mela and for whom I endured the noisy crowds and chaos of the fair on a beach, where sand got into anything you ate and everything you wore, this child was going to go away to make her own home and live with another family. I could hardly think of it. Yet, it was happening. Time was moving on with or without me, and I was left sitting in a train, travelling from station to station, while my daughter was getting ready for a life-changing journey. Without me by her side.

I clearly remember that as I was handing over the money to Amina, I felt immensely relieved and a little less guilty about not being there, not present, to do some of the many things that had to be done. It did not relieve me of the heavy weight of an impending parting, though.

Sometimes, I think I keep a record in my head of the things I could do and the things I could not do as a father. That does not mean that the things done make up for those not done. It's just that I like to think that whenever it was possible, in little ways or big ones, I tried to let my children know that their wants and desires mattered to me. They matter to me.

I had made many trips to Paris and was familiar with the city. When I started travelling for concerts with my sons, I would do my best to see that they were comfortable and enjoyed their trip. On one particular trip, I remember well, my sons were complaining that they were fed up of eating the bland hotel food. They were craving the flavours of home, the taste, fragrance and feel of roti, parantha, masala, curry, dal! Even the style of eating this food is so different. The joy of eating with your hands, tearing off bits of roti or naan with your fingers, wrapping a bit of tikka or kebab in them or dipping them into a thick gravy—those of us who are used to eating like this find it hard to forget or leave behind the experience for too long. These young men were the same infants and children whom, once, I had fed with my own hands. It does not feel like such a long time ago.

One day, when I could see that they could take it no more, I decided to surprise them. I told them to come with me for a walk around the city, and gradually led them through the inner roads and bylanes to a small restaurant that was owned by a Pakistani. When they saw where we had arrived, they jumped with joy, they hugged me and I think they would have even danced a little bit were they of such nature. The contentment and satisfaction I saw on their faces, after eating in that tiny restaurant in a remote bylane of Paris, was simply priceless.

Here is another Paris story of one such last minute fiasco. We were running late. Since I knew that the organizers and the audiences in Paris were very punctual, I told my sons,

Murtuza and Qadir, who were also going to perform with me in the show, to hurry. In that rush, we quickly left with our instruments for the venue. Paris has very heavy traffic and it took us two hours to cover the short distance in a car.

We were finally inside the green room and getting ready when the laundry man came to take our clothes for ironing. This is when my sons realized that they had left our performance attire at the hotel. I felt very angry and a little anxious, and told them to go and get the clothes as quickly as possible as the show was going to start in less than half an hour. They left immediately, but I realized that it was just not possible for them to go and come back in the time we had. Imagine my surprise, relief and joy when I saw them back with our clothes within fifteen minutes! They had decided to simply walk the distance and after getting directions from the driver, they were off, jogging through Paris. When I asked them how they managed it, they laughed happily and told me, quite proudly, that they took a shortcut! They ran down the streets and back alleys that only local people know, and returned the same way. They were just barely out of breath. Perhaps that is because of the breathing techniques and exercises that have been a part of their training over the years.

I know I do not talk much of these things. These stories are a part of who I am. Once we started travelling as a family of musicians and performers, it became difficult for me to even remember the times when I travelled alone. Those times, now long past, seem to be a part of someone else's life, not mine. I have grown very used to having my sons around me for concerts. That is how it has been for decades now.

They all started very young. They trained very well; they became calm, experienced and quick to find solutions to the many problems that happen at the last minute. Travelling together, my children and I have been each other's back-up and support in many different ways, some of them quite funny. There was this time in London, when after the performance, we decided to go shopping. We were to fly back to India early the next morning. We were so engrossed in shopping that we forgot all about the time and had to rush back to our hotel to pack our bags for the early morning flight.

Next morning, when we reached the airport, the customs people stopped Murtuza for carrying excess baggage. How much excess baggage? He was carrying over one hundred kilos! I couldn't believe this, and I told the man at the customs check that my son would pay for his excess baggage himself. Hearing this, Murtuza looked upset and seeing the look on his face, I could not help but laugh. Of course, I paid. Even the man at the customs check was laughing when he realized we were family.

Disciples and Teachers

One might imagine that in the old days, a teacher sat with a circle of disciples under the calm shade of a tree and taught them the wisdom that was his to teach. Today, there is noise, there are rooms, there is traffic, and even the world of teacher and disciple looks different in image, expectation and character. Yet, when I think of these things, I understand that the calm shade of a tree might still be allowed to persist and sustain us if we understand the spirit of this relationship. The calm and the shade are for us to hold in heart and mind, and most importantly, in the respect we bear towards each other, both as teacher and as student. No relationship is a one-way road.

I have always consciously endeavoured to treat all my disciples with the love and regard that a teacher must have for all his pupils. There is no room for inequality in attitude or behaviour, and I am not influenced by the social status of anyone. I have had many pupils who were celebrities in their own right and had their own fan following. Hariharan, Sonu Nigam, A.R. Rahman, Shaan and many others are all great musicians. They have a circle of fans and supporters much larger than mine and are perhaps known more widely than I am. To their credit, they have all only given me immense love and respect. They have treated me like their guru and an elder. In turn, I have imparted whatever musical knowledge I could to them and loved them like my own children.

Although I am very proud of each of my disciples, I have never let their star status and their generosity of acknowledging me as their guru go to my head. I consider myself a teacher and I am grateful if I have been able to help them in any way I could. Ego and conceit are the biggest enemies of an artiste. Humility takes you closer to God. One should be true to one's art and leave everything else to the Almighty. You may think that these are easy words to speak and there is nobody to say or see who you are in your heart, the truth about you as a person. But there is always God who sees us as we are; nothing is hidden from Him. Once this is clear, then it becomes easier to see how each of us has our own potential, our own little points of weakness and our own great strengths. There are things that we all pray for and those prayers only God can hear. If I understand this about myself, I can understand this about every other person.

I was chosen to receive the Dinanath Mangeshkar Award in the year 2011. At the award function, before presenting the award to me, the great Bharat Ratna, Lata Mangeshkar, said to the audience, 'Ustadji is my guru also, in a way. There was a difficult time when my throat was not supporting my voice and I started getting quite upset and scared at my inability to sing properly. At that time, I went to Ustadji and told him my problem. He said not to worry, and said that there are such times in every singer's life. He, then, taught me a new music composition that helped me overcome my problem and sing again.'

There was loud applause from the audience when she said this and it made me happy to have been so acknowledged. While we were leaving the venue after the event, a close friend asked me, 'Why didn't you tell me that you have coached the great Lata Mangeshkar? Now that she has publicly acknowledged you as her guru, why don't you add her name to your list of students?'

I looked at him, but I did not answer because the explanation seemed too complicated, perhaps even too philosophical. He, however, demanded an answer.

So I told him what I truly felt, 'Lata Mangeshkar is a world renowned singer and the nightingale of India. She is a Bharat Ratna. It is her greatness, not mine, that she has publicly acknowledged me and given me the stature of being her guru.'

My friend looked at me and I saw the amazement in his eyes. I suppose I thought that being so close to me, he should be knowing me better by now. I am grateful to God for my place in this world and for the relationships I have had with others—students, friends, other musicians, my own family, my children, who too have been my students and now perform with me. These are not for sale, or to be used to increase some false sense of a market value. These are all people and experiences to be cherished.

I have spent a lot of time thinking about music and the quality of various kinds of voices in my life. I have done some homework and research of my own on the subject. I am amazed by the fact that each of my students sings in three octaves. It is difficult for people to expand their vocal range, though I know that with riyaz and guidance, you can expand it. This is a gift from Allah, to me and to them. Even their voice and pitch levels are right for hitting precise notes. Not one of my students sings in a falsetto—a voice that is artificially high.

I am often asked by my students and by others to give words of advice to an aspiring singer or musician. Perhaps this is the right place to share some such beliefs with you. You may take it as advice. You may choose to simply accept it as my way. Do your music lessons, do your scales, even if it irritates you to repeat them and repeat them again. Do not underestimate the scales. Yes, I hated the scales too. I did them not always very happily, so I understand why many singers get tired of practising the scales. They are crucial to training your voice and equally crucial to training your ear. They are the basis of expertise in technique.

Practice, practice, practice. Open your mind and listen to all types of music—classic rock, the classics, jazz, the blues, country, blue grass, hip hop, R&B, reggae, ambient, house/techno/electronic, alternative, remixes and yes, even 'top 40'.

Do not be afraid. Dismiss nothing.

If music is your craft, drown yourself in it seriously. Follow your heart, but have a backup plan. Music is perhaps one of the greatest activities of human creation. Do not assume that 'your' music is better or is everything that may 'really' be called music. Respect everyone's music as much as you can. There is no reason to feel obliged to like everything that you hear, but hear it with respect. Somebody likes that music. It connects with the soul and life experiences of another person.

Every artiste's path is unique. Hearing another person's story of success can be motivating, but your story is your own.

Be present and engaged with what is in front of you today and do not live in the future, waiting for something that may or may not come. Wishing your life away is much more tragic than finding fulfilment by doing what you love today, right where you are!

Hamare buzurg yeh bolte the, koi bhi kaam creation ka aisa hota hai, jisme lagi toh rozi nahi toh roza (Our elders used to say, creative work is like this—if you get work you eat, if you do not, you starve). *Isliye backup plan hona chahiye* (So you should have a backup plan).

Sapne dekho, lekin unke poore hone ki shart mat rakho (Dream your dreams, but do not bet on them coming true).

Khushboo bano! Khushboo ko kitna bhi koi bottle main band kare, woh aati zaroor hai (Be like a fragrance. You cannot trap fragrance in a bottle, fragrance will spread).

All I am saying is, do not lose the dream, but be practical, and always do the good that is possible for you to do. That is the greatest gift you can give to anyone. That is your gratitude to God.

Papa teaches music to his students sitting on a carpet on the floor. He has been doing this for many, many years.

Once, when Papa was out of town for a concert, Ammi decided to do some spring cleaning. She called in some help to roll up the thick carpet so that it could be dusted and aired, and the floor underneath could be scrubbed and disinfected. She wanted the room spruced up before Papa returned from his tour and took it over again. She was sure that Papa would appreciate her doing this and praise her, as he always did, for all her efforts to take care of him.

As the thick carpet was rolled up, she got the shock of her life. There was money under the carpet. Shock turned into a delighted laugh. She could not believe this was how he saved his money. Since Papa was not in town, she could not even ask him about it. So she put the money away and decided to ask Papa later why he chose this strange place instead of a wallet or a savings envelope.

When Papa returned home after a couple of days, the first thing that Ammi asked him about was the cash that was discovered under the carpet. My goodness, you should have seen the stunned look on his face. His expression changed from shock to irritation and then to one of helpless resignation at realizing that his secret piggy bank was no longer a secret.

He sat down with the guilty but endearing look of a little boy who has been caught. Upon repeated entreaties from his wife and playful ribbing from all of us, he finally disclosed that he would keep some money as his personal savings under the carpet out of the money that he allocated for household expenses to give to Ammi.

When we teased him about it and Ammi sulked at this revelation, he told us that he did this because he did not want to ask his wife for money repeatedly. Ammi asked him what he used his savings for, and though at first, he was silent, he looked her in the eye and said, 'My personal savings give me the freedom of doing exactly as I please without asking anyone or telling anyone anything.'

'But what did you wish to do with this money?' Ammi asked him in jest.

He answered with great seriousness, 'To give to various charities that I have adopted over the years, to donate at the mosque for the aid and medical treatment of the poor, and to have a little money with me to buy something, as and when I want to, for my children and grandchildren—without asking you for it.'

As he said this, all of us were overwhelmed by emotion and I found I had tears in my eyes. Here is another side of Papa. His philanthropy. What had started out as a funny incident for us, with us relishing the idea of teasing Papa, ended with all of us looking a little weepy. He looked at our faces and laughed, then waved us all away as if he no longer wished to speak of this. 'Go on now; don't you have work to do? Shame on you, troubling me!'

As I watched his childlike expressions during the telling of his story, my mind wandered to the old tale of the piggy bank created by his mother in a hole in the wall. A place where a little boy knew there would always be the coins his mother saved and shared with him, until the terrible day that he found it empty. Wall, floor, under the carpet—we all need to know that we can dip in there on a rainy day, for our families, for those who need help and for ourselves. Papa's humanness makes it very easy for any of us to connect easily and comfortably with him.

This same man has travelled the world, mingled with celebrities and performed before royalty. He sang at the Golden Jubilee celebrations in the presence of Queen Elizabeth II in the UK in 2002. He sang at the Festival de Lille in the presence of Lady Diana in France. He performed at Baltimore University and was conferred an Honorary Citizenship of Baltimore City. The Governor of

Maryland presented him with Honorary Citizenship for outstanding contribution to the field of Indian classical music in 1986.

He is someone who has visited the UK so frequently that he knows all the little byways and narrow lanes of London—so well, in fact, that many who have lived there, been born and brought up there, do not know the city as well as he does. He was once at the home of a friend of his called Ismail Shaikh, where two of his students, Rupal and Tina, had come to meet him. When they arrived, he asked them to take him for a drive to Southall, thinking they would know where it was. He was quite surprised to learn that they had no clue! Therefore, he gave them directions and they drove him there.

He is the same man who, long ago, went with a large contingent of singers and musicians to perform at a show where the chief guest was Marie Jose. She was the queen of Italy for a while, the last queen of that country. She liked his performance so much that she showered him with praise and affection, saying, 'From today, you are my son.' She honoured him with her card—not something that was given to everyone. Papa handed the card over for safekeeping to one of the organizers. Later, this person flatly refused all memory of having been given the card, and I assume he kept it for himself as a treasured souvenir.

He never tells anyone when he helps someone out or donates to a cause. We only come to know of these things sometimes, and by accident. Once, through a student, he sent a money order to a relative who was in financial difficulty. The address on the money order was of Papa's family house in Badaun instead of the address of the person to whom he was sending the money. As it happens, Murtuza bhai was there at the time. He was overseeing some construction and renovation work on the old house. Therefore, when the postman came, he delivered the money order into Bhai's hands. Bhai looked at it and immediately called Papa to ask him what he was to do with it. Papa was quite upset. He asked Murtuza to return the money order. It was only much later that we realized it must have been for a relative. He never spoke to us about it.

Part of the faith others have in him is that he will never break the confidence of another. If someone is in need, there is always a sense of anxiety for what others may think if they find out. Papa has never let on when he has known that a friend, a relative or a student has needed money, and he has never let anyone know when he has responded by helping someone out.

He still does not reveal anything of the charity and philanthropic help he extends to others. It is only between him and Almighty Allah.

Friends and Fans

A.R. Rahman

I had first heard about Ustadji from Hariharan. I remember I had asked him, 'Who are you getting trained under?' and he had replied, 'all that I am, is because of Ustad Ghulam Mustafa Khan.' That is how I discovered Khan sahib.

When I met his family, I realized they were completely immersed in music. There is so much distraction in the world, but he and his family single-mindedly focus on music, and as a consequence have nurtured many singers. Khan sahib has passed on a rich musical tradition to his grandchildren. Oh! How his grandson Faiz Mustafa Khan sang in *Coke Studio* with us! I was amazed! We should salute Khan sahib for contributing so much to his family, India, and the world through his music.

As a teacher, I feel knowledge is transferred from one heart to another; it is not only physical, but also a dua and a spiritual connection.

Khan sahib is one of the best human beings I have ever come across. He has a positive attitude towards life and always wants to teach and share his knowledge. He rarely wants anything in return, which is one great thing I have learnt from him.

* * *

Ustad Zakir Hussain

My childhood was spent in the company of Ustad Ghulam Mustafa Khan. I am forever indebted and grateful to him for providing me with the opportunity to accompany him on the tabla when he recorded his first LP. I was still in school then, and though more experienced and famous tabla players were available and ready to perform with him, he gave me the opportunity to do so. It was a great honour for me.

I remember going for the recording in my school uniform, carrying the tablas in my arms. It was also my first ever recording as a classical musician, and I was elated. This was indeed a big occasion for me and I am grateful to the Almighty that I got to play with a great master like Ustad Ghulam Mustafa Khan sahib. I am also thankful to him for recommending my name to other musicians.

He sang Raag Bageshwari, and he sang it with such preparation and clarity that it was simply mind-blowing. I wonder if anybody else could have sung it so clearly. His music could consume you completely and you could get lost in it. His riyaz and preparation were always perfect, and one could never detect a false note in Khan sahib's singing. It was an education in itself for me to listen to him from such close quarters and to accompany him on the tabla.

Some twenty years later, in 1980, I was playing with a very famous and renowned Hindustani classical singer, whom I cannot name here, and Ustad Ghulam Mustafa Khan's name came up for discussion. I was stunned by what the man said to me about Khan sahib. He said, 'When I heard Ghulam Mustafa Khan, believe me, I did not eat for the next three days, wondering what I was doing next to a singer like him.' Such is the awe and admiration that his peers have for him.

Ustad Ghulam Mustafa Khan sahib is a saint of a man. He never talks about himself and remains simple and humble to the core, even after so much acclaim, honour and fan following.

For him, his world is his music, his riyaz and his family.

* * *

Waheeda Rehman

Some forty-five years ago, when I was already an established actor, I had this desire to learn music but could not find a suitable guru. One day, a friend of mine suggested the name of Ustad Ghulam Mustafa Khan and told me that he was the best person to learn music from. I got in touch with Khan sahib and he very kindly agreed to be my teacher. He used to come to my house to teach me and sometimes, when I did not have a shoot schedule, I used to go to his house to learn from him.

I remember him telling me on day one of my training that I required a good harmonium, so I bought one and we started training. Just three months later, on 27 April 1974, I got married to Shashi and moved to Bangalore. Life went on and I had my two children, Sohail and Kashvi. My married life and bringing up my children kept me totally occupied, and it was not until my husband's death in 2001 that I returned to Mumbai, to my Bandra house.

Suddenly, after a gap of almost twenty-seven years, I thought about resuming my music training. Immediately, I again thought about guruji. I still had his old telephone number and I took a chance and dialled it, hoping against hope that it had not changed. As luck would have it, it had not. I was thrilled to hear his voice at the other end and requested him to once again take me under his tutelage and resume my music training. The good man that he is, he readily agreed to do so and my training began again in right earnest.

One day, I asked him what he thought about my voice and asked him to tell me frankly if I was any good. He smiled and told me that my voice was very good, and that he would one day make me sing a song from one of my films and record it too. I was quite thrilled at hearing that and thanked him for his praise.

The one thing I find amazing and highly admirable in Ustadji is his patience and his capacity to give unconditional love to his students. He works very hard with each student and is genuinely desirous of imparting his knowledge to his students. It was much later that I learnt that great singers and musicians like A.R. Rahman, Sonu Nigam, Hariharan and Shaan were also his students. I regret that I have not been able to learn music from him properly, but promise to become his student again in my next birth, if possible, so that I can be a better disciple.

I was delighted to see him on television, receiving his Padma Vibhushan from the President of India. I called him up and congratulated him on being awarded the second highest civilian honour of India. I wish him good health and even more success.

* * *

Hariharan

It was in 1974 that I heard my guruji, Ustad Ghulam Mustafa Khan, for the first time. It was also the first time that I was listening to Raag Bageshwari and Bhopal todi, and I was simply astounded. That day, I became a big fan of Khan sahib. I fell in love with his singing and vowed to myself that I would learn the intricacies of music from him.

When I came home that day, I told my mother about my decision. Quite surprised at my overconfidence and presumptuousness, she asked me whether I knew of Khan sahib's stature and respect in the world of music. She expressed her apprehensions about whether Khan sahib would agree to take me as his student. However, I was undeterred. I had decided, and there was no way I was going to be dissuaded from my yearning to learn music from the great master. I told my mother that if I were fortunate, Ustadji would heed my request and agree to teach me.

Sometime later, I was at a party with my mother where the greats of Indian music, like Ustad Amir Khan sahib, Ustad Allah Rakha sahib, Ustad Halim Jaffar Khan sahib and others were present. At some point during the party, I found myself standing near them, completely awestruck, when I noticed a younger gentleman humming to himself. I looked closely and realized that it was none other than my idol, Ustad Ghulam Mustafa Khan sahib. I was delighted at the opportunity that had presented itself and started following him around at the party, but could not muster enough courage to actually go across to him and meet him.

A few days later, at another event, my mother and I found ourselves sitting right next to Khan sahib. I was super excited at seeing him sitting so close to us and told my mother I must speak to him. Gathering all my courage, I approached him nervously. After greeting him appropriately, I, without any preamble, blurted out to him that I wanted to sing and that I wanted him to teach me. Khan sahib looked at me closely and smiled.

His smile gave me confidence—I told him that I stayed nearby and it would be my pleasure if he could come to our house for a cup of coffee. To my delight and good fortune, Khan sahib agreed.

When we reached home, Khan sahib gently asked me to sing something for him. He said, 'If you want to learn music from me, show me how you sing.' I found merit in what Khan sahib was saying, but in my nervousness, my hands were shaking at the thought of singing in front of him.

Nevertheless, I somehow managed to sing something. He heard me patiently; after I had finished, he gave me his home address and told me to come to his home the day after. You can imagine my joy at being accepted as his student.

That is how I started training under Khan sahib. The one discipline that he insisted on was regular riyaz (practice). He told me, 'Always do riyaz. Whatever you learn, practise it. It is only repeated practice that makes a song. If you only learn the song, it will remain in your head and after some time, evaporate from your head. Unless the song settles down in your throat, the voice will not support it.'

* * *

Sonu Nigam

Whenever Ustad Ghulam Mustafa Khan's name is mentioned, there is a sense of peace that envelopes my heart and soul. A flash of light is sparked in my mind. Khan sahib has dedicated his entire life to music. Not only has he set a benchmark of knowledge, he has also enlightened many students like me by keeping his hand on our heads and blessing us.

The first time I saw Ustadji was on the *Sa Re Ga Ma Pa* show that I was hosting on TV. The moment I looked at him, there was a voice inside me that told me that I had found my teacher. I felt that I must learn music from him. As I looked at his face, I could see the glow and radiance that you normally see in an enlightened man's face. There was this peace and serenity of expression that I cannot describe in words. I longed for him to accept me as a pupil and teach me music.

I started learning music from guruji in 1997, and whatever he taught me, or whatever I could learn from him, changed my entire way of singing and of doing riyaz. With his hand on my head, my approach to and understanding of music changed and I realized that I had a huge distance to cover.

Many people teach music, but what is unique about Ustadji is that he teaches you voice culture. It is only because of guruji that I have been able to reach the place I am at today. Had it not been for him, I would not have been able to sing half as well as I sing today.

Guruji is one man who has never indulged in PR, publicity or manipulation. He has also never really craved the limelight. His has been a single-minded devotion to his music.

I am grateful to God that I was able to meet such a fine human being and was able to learn music from him.

* * *

Mashkoor Hussain

Ustad Ghulam Mustafa Khan is my brother-in-law. The incidents that I am going to narrate to you here highlight the care and understanding with which he has always treated other artistes, and how he has never rebuked or undermined any other musician for any of their shortcomings or mistakes.

To elucidate my point, I want to tell you about an incident that took place in Bihar a long time ago. Ustad sahib was to perform at a show in Gaya. I was travelling with him. Unfortunately, the tabla player, who is an essential accompanist for any singer, could not be finalized. As the show was about to start, we decided to engage a local tabla player and Ustad sahib told us that he would manage. What we did not realize was that this tabla player was a novice and did not know even the ABC of music or beats. The entire performance was marred because of his inability to match beats with Ustad sahib. Instead of getting angry or refusing to perform, Khan sahib somehow managed to sing and complete his performance as planned. The audience was unaware of what a difficult task it was for him to perform with an accompanist who was a novice and was playing his instrument, in this case the tabla, poorly. Even after the show ended, he refused to say anything to the tabla player, or reprimand him for playing poorly, because of his belief that no artiste should be humiliated and that all artistes need to be respected.

I recall another incident. We were in Toronto, Canada, when an Indian singer, who lived there, kept pestering us to let him meet Ustad sahib as he was a fan of his. We kept telling him that the schedule was very tight and that it may not be possible for us to organize a meeting for him, but he persisted. At last, we requested Ustad sahib to spare some time and he generously agreed to do so, asking us to invite the gentleman over in the evening.

When the man arrived, we were horrified to see that instead of greeting Ustad sahib or trying to speak to him, he rushed straight to the kitchen and got hold of a metal plate and spoon. He came out beating these against each other and started singing loudly to display his singing talent in front of the master! Alas, making matters worse, he was completely out of tune. Here again, the great patience and compassion of Ustad sahib rescued the situation for us all. He heard him out patiently and instead of telling him that he sang out of tune, or that he was a bad singer, he praised him. Then he gently asked him to practise more—all this because of his rule of never humiliating an artiste and encouraging singers.

This is my brother-in-law—a man with a compassionate understanding of human nature. It would be easy for a person of his stature and accomplishments to be dismissive, to keep his time and his space to himself, to express irritation at the enthusiastic and often impolite behaviour that we all often encounter, but he has never done so. He has remained unfailingly patient with the people around him.

* * *

Shaan

I had always heard from my father, Manas Mukherjee, who was a fan of Ustadji, about what a great singer he was, but I only got the opportunity to meet him much later. This was when I went to his house with Mr Gajendra Singh while I was hosting the famous music show, *Sa Re Ga Ma Pa* on TV.

I always tell everyone that guruji not only teaches music, he teaches how to live life. He teaches us how to treat others with respect, the importance of relationships and how to handle them. He teaches us how to be good human beings.

Along the way, while you are busy imbibing all these virtues from him, he quietly also teaches you music.

For all the seriousness of Shaan's words and feelings for Papa, I cannot help but share a lovely and funny incident involving the two of them and Radhika, Shaan's wife. Once, Papa was in a playful mood and light-heartedly told Shaan, his student, that he was in the mood to have tea at his house.

A little surprised at this sudden request, Shaan immediately complied and took Papa to his house. Radhika was not at home at this time, so he gallantly decided to make the tea for Papa himself.

Once the tea was made, both sat down to drink it. Papa went through his cup slowly as they discussed music. Then

Radhika returned home. She greeted Papa with great respect and affection and asked him if she could get him anything to eat.

Papa said, 'Bahu, main tumhare haath ki chai peena chahta hoon (I want to drink tea made by you. 'Bahu' means daughter-in-law).'

Shaan was nonplussed at hearing this and said, 'Ustadji, maine abhi toh aap ke liye chai banayi hai (Ustadji, but I just made tea for you).'

Papa smiled and said, 'Jo maine pehle piya tha woh tumhara pyaar tha, ab main chai peena chahta hoon (What I drank earlier was made with your love, now I want to drink some real tea).'

Shaan stared at him and Radhika laughed. Papa smiled at Shaan, that familiar, almost naughty, twinkle in his eyes, and Shaan too burst out laughing.

There are many reasons why Papa's students adore him. His humour is as much one of those reasons as his great understanding of music. This ready humour holds together the relationships and people that surround him. On a normal day, this is a normal part of all our interactions with him. Sometimes, when things are a little difficult or stressful, his ability to lighten overwrought moods and feelings seems to bring all situations within the realm of resolution.

Swaroop Bhalwanker

I am the son of the assistant commissioner of Mumbai. I know I am a spoilt brat, not at all musically inclined. My father wanted me to learn music as he was a tabla player. In 2003, I became a student of Ustad Ghulam Mustafa Khan.

More than music, I learnt how to live life and how to handle my life. I would keep the company of wrong people and had bad habits, like being unpunctual, uncultured and having no discipline.

Guruji taught and trained me how to be a good student and a good human being. For the first six months, I was not at all serious, not punctual, did not dress appropriately and had no dedication. So he used to send me back, that is, not teach me on the days that I did not follow the rules and etiquette. Then one day, I saw Shaan, Sonu Nigam, Hariharan bhai and other such great singers and artistes all arriving on time; I was the only one who came in late. This made me think a little.

After sometime, friends who knew I had joined music classes asked me, '*Arey, kya seekh raha hai aaj kal* (What are you learning these days)?' I laughed and said, '*Time par aana seekha hai* (I have learnt how to be on time).'

I was a lefty—left-handed—but guruji said, '*Hamare yahan left se nahi right hand se baja bajana sikhate hain* (we teach how to play instruments with the right hand, not the left), so he taught me how to use my right hand. Today, this benefits me as I use both my left and right hands.

These experiences have helped me grow as a person. He taught me to wear proper clothes, talk properly, and my attitude changed.

Ek woh waqt tha (There was that time)! *Aur aaj yeh waqt hai* (And then there is today), when guruji likes spending time with me. *Main yeh nahin bol sakta ki woh mere dost hain, meri itni aukaat nahi hai* (I cannot say he is my friend, for I am not at that stature). However, I feel he has all that fun with me now that he could not have in his younger days due to shows, riyaz, responsibilities and difficulties. I take him for long drives, to eat ice cream and pani puri. He spends most of the time talking about spirituality.

Once, we went to watch *Bal Gandharva* in a small city theatre. It is a musical film. The theatre was empty as no one had bought tickets and they were planning to cancel that show. Because guruji wanted to watch the film, I bought ten tickets so that the film was played as per the schedule. When we entered the theatre, it was dark, as the show was about to start. Innocently, guruji said loudly, '*Arey, light on karo, hum movie dekhne aaye hain* (switch on the lights, we're here to watch the movie).' That day I realized how passionate he was about music—*ki unko yeh bhi nahi pata ki theatre ki light off ho jati hain movie chalu hote waqt* (he doesnt even know that lights go off before a movie show). The movie started and after sometime, he asked, '*Beta, yeh jo chhota sa bachcha hai, yahi Bal Gandharva hai kya asli mein* (Tell me son, this little child, is he the real Bal Gandharva)?' I answered, '*Nahi guruji, yeh acting kar raha hai us character ki* (No guruji, the child is an actor playing the character).'

While he was talking, he was quite loud, and a few people who had joined in later to watch the same movie started yelling, '*Arey dheere se baat karo, hum bhi movie dekhne aaye hain* (Talk softly! We are also hereto watch the movie)!' During the interval, when the lights were switched on, those people behind us saw and recognized Ustadji. They were very happy and surprised. They apologized and started seeking his blessings. So guruji said, '*Arey maafi tumlog kyun maang rahe ho, maafi to mujhe maangi chahiye ki aap logon ko disturb kiya picture dekhte waqt* (Why are you apologizing? I am the one who has to apologize for disturbing you during the show)!'

* * *

Rachana Shah

I learnt music from my maternal uncle, Hridaynath Mangeshkar, the famous singer and music director, for about three to four years. One day, he told me that I was not taking my training seriously as he was my uncle, and that I was taking too many things for granted. He told me that if I really wanted to learn music, I should learn it from a good guru, one who was not related to me. He said that would only happen if I stepped outside my house and that he could think of no better teacher, who had the required expertise and stature, the respect of all who knew him, than the famous Hindustani classical maestro, Ustad Ghulam Mustafa Khan.

I asked my uncle if such a famous personality would be willing to teach me. He gave me Khan sahib's phone number and told me that he had never, till date, met a man who had his humility, who was as encouraging and kind.

When I called Ustadji, I was delighted to hear him tell me to come over to his house the next day at 11 a.m. My heart full of happiness, I ran to my aunt, Lata didi, and told her the good news. She was as excited to hear the news as I was, and told me, 'Oh my God, you are really blessed if he has agreed to teach you. Go ahead. I am very happy and proud that he is teaching you.'

The next morning, to make sure that I reached on time for my first class, I ended up reaching his building five minutes before time. My mother was accompanying me. We waited till 11 a.m. and I rang the doorbell exactly at the appointed hour. His daughter, Nazma opened the door and graciously welcomed us in, telling me that Ustadji was waiting for me.

As I entered, I saw that a tanpura had already been laid out, and the first question that Ustadji asked me was if I knew how to play the instrument. When I replied in the affirmative, he asked me to play and after listening for some time, he told me it was perfect. Then he asked me to sing something because he wanted to understand what I already knew. I decided to sing a Marathi bandish for him. After I had finished singing, he told me that he loved my voice and then, looking at my mother, he told her that he was confident of taking me ahead. I was on cloud nine that day.

After that, I started going to him once a week or at times, twice a week too, depending upon the engagements and shows he had. Despite his hectic schedule and travelling, he made sure that he spared some time to teach me. He was kind enough to teach me many bandishes and *raagdaris*.

Ustadji used to be forever concerned about my health because I looked so thin and scrawny. He would always ask me if I had eaten. Whenever I went to his house, he always made sure that I was served a cup of hot milk as soon I entered because he felt that I was too weak to take on the rigours of riyaz, because of my physical appearance.

Ustadji and Lata didi used to keep talking about my progress and Ustadji kept her updated on my training. During the time that I was learning music from him, he never made me feel that he was a celebrity. He was kind towards me and encouraged me a lot. He always treated me as though he knew what I was doing and he never shouted at me or reprimanded me if I did something incorrectly. He would keep quiet and patiently wait for me to finish before giving me some tips and asking me to repeat the song or exercise. He is one of the finest teachers one can have. Whatever he teaches about a raag, he demonstrates it practically for the student so that they can understand the finer nuances. Usually, either a teacher is good in theory or in practical singing, but a man who is a master of both is of immense help when a student is trying to grapple with the intricacies of raags, etc. That is exactly what Ustadji is—a master of both theory and practice—and that is a unique combination. Not all singers are great teachers. Frankly, teaching is one art and singing is another, so if one can find a teacher who has the DNA of both, nothing can be better.

He and his family welcomed me into their hearts and home as if I were one of them, and never let me feel like just a student or an outsider. I regret that I could not remain a part of that wonderful family longer, because I got married and had to give up learning music. How I wish I could have continued.

Ustadji is a rare combination of confidence and humility. I call his expertise at singing his innate talent. It comes so naturally to him, it is as if he was born with it. And here, I am not disputing the long years of riyaz and dedication that he must have endured to reach this point, where it seems that it all flows naturally from him.

For an artiste to be great, his heart has to be in the right place, because that is what sets him apart and allows him to leave an indelible impression on whoever comes in contact with him. Ustadji is one such person and that is the secret of the magic he continues to create. His innate 'niceness' flows through his music, which is why whenever you hear him sing, everything else fades away and you are left with a sense of mellifluous peace.

I cannot relate any funny incidents from my training with him simply because I was too much in awe of him. The only thing I do remember is that I used to start laughing whenever I made a mistake and used to find him joining in before he ultimately corrected me. That space that he provided to me really helped my confidence.

One day, he asked me, 'Rachana beta, since you come from a renowned, music family yourself, I want to ask you what they said when you decided to learn music from me.'

I smiled at him and told him that it was not I who decided, but my family, that there could be no better teacher for me than him. It is a big thing when a music family decides to send one from their own family to someone outside to learn music from.

It shows their appreciation and regard for the ustad as well as the confidence they have in his teaching.

Lata didi and Ustadji are great friends and she has the utmost respect for him, just as he has for her. His soul is completely immersed in music and that is going to remain eternal. His is not a name that is ever going to be forgotten.

He is so grounded and dedicated to his music that the highs and the lows of life have not affected him, and he remains at his peak always.

It is when one talks about people like Ustad Ghulam Mustafa Khan that one can safely say 'Good does not come with an expiry date'.

While working on the stories in this book, I have found that there are aspects of Papa that have reached the stature of a legend, like the patience, the respect and the dignity he accords to other artistes. I know that we have sometimes asked him how it is that he is able to maintain both good humour as well as his calm when someone behaves badly or foolishly around him, disturbs the atmosphere or messes up something they are supposed to do. He responds with one of his favourite quotes from the poetry and writings of the last Mughal emperor, Bahadur Shah Zafar. It is this:

Na thi haal ki jab humein apni khabar, rahe dekhte auron ke aib-o-hunar

Padi apni buraaiyon pe jo nazar, to nigaah mein koi buraa na raha

(When you are self-aware, you are in no state to comment on another's faults or brilliance

When you recognize your own shortcomings, then nobody can be seen as a bad person.)

When I embarked upon this ambitious project of co-writing the autobiography of Ustad Ghulam Mustafa Khan, my dear father-in-law, whom I call my Papa, and who is a maestro of Hindustani classical music, I never imagined that it would be so difficult.

I thought I would research and sit down with Papa to speak to him about his life, his experiences, his achievements, his moments of pride and his disappointments, and that by the end of it, I would have a document that, in the sharing, would do justice to his life and the beliefs that make him who he is. What I did not anticipate was that Papa is not a man who likes to talk much about himself. How does one compile the autobiography of a man who is so self-effacing, so modest and so untouched by glitz, glamour or by his formidable accomplishments, that he doesn't feel the need to tell his story to the world, or sometimes even to his own family? How does one compel a man, who does not consider himself a celebrity, to talk about his achievements and the honours that have been bestowed on him?

You cannot compel such a man to do anything. That is the truth and the only answer. Therefore, I simply spent hours listening. This I have learnt from him. Listen, he always says, because listening is a large part of learning. I know he is talking about music, but I think that the advice holds true for most things in life. What you have read in these pages is the result of my persistent efforts to jog his memory, ask him questions, get him to tell me stories, answer questions, bridge gaps and just generally not give up on the project! His legendary patience has stood me in good stead. I know there have been times that I have driven him to the point of great irritation, because I could not understand something—either the connection between things so clear in his head, or the spirit behind a story that makes it important to him. Yet, he has remained affectionate and generous with his time and energy because he accepts that this, his autobiography, is important to me, to each member of his family, and to the many people who love and respect him.

As a co-writer, I have played the role of the other party in conversation with Ustad Ghulam Mustafa Khan. I have done my best to record what he has communicated about his life, the content and the spirit and feelings behind that content.

Even though he has been honoured with the Padma Vibhushan, the country's second highest civilian honour, and he may one day, by the grace of God, be awarded the highest honour, the Bharat Ratna, which many feel he should have already received, he remains a man who practises enormous humility. Not for a moment can one detect any indication of him being so influenced or affected by the accolades and praise, that he changes in any of those beloved aspects that are so essential to his personality and his music.

He remains totally devoted and dedicated to his craft. For him, his life is his riyaz, his students and his family, which includes his own family and the extended family comprised of his well-wishers, supporters and fans.

Every so often, when I would press him to sit with me and tell me something about his life so that it could be included in his autobiography, he would ask me with great seriousness, 'Why would anyone be interested in knowing about my life? Do you really think people would be interested in buying a book to read about an ordinary man's life?'

That is what he believes he is, an ordinary man, one among other ordinary human beings. While many people are amazed at this approach of his to his life, wondering whether he is for real, whether this is a false sense of modesty, I would like to say that this is simply him. I believe with all my heart that his wisdom and compassion come from his ability to connect deeply with what many of us dismiss as the ordinary. Papa is dismissive of nothing in daily life, he has the ability to value rain, pakoras, ice cream, the first fruit of the season that appears on a tree, a child's gift of a far-from-perfect roti, or a terrifyingly enthusiastic, even if a little rude, singer who bangs a spoon against a plate in a misplaced attempt to seek his attention and praise. A job, for a person who seeks to sustain himself to pursue a passion— Papa understands these ordinary things. That is what makes him extraordinary and that is what raises his interactions in life, with everyone around him, to the level of the most extraordinary.

Ustad Ghulam Mustafa Khan is a rare sort of person. If I seek to remind him of his achievements, the name that he has made for himself in the field of Hindustani classical music, and the honours that he has received, he simply says, 'Yeh sab Allah ki meherbani hai (This is all God's grace). What have I done to deserve this honour, love and affection? I have only followed my path devotedly and am happy that I have been able to share what I know with my students.'

Besides being a doyen of Hindustani classical music, he is known and respected by the world as a great teacher who has imparted his knowledge to many people, and those people are now themselves respected as masters and celebrities in the field of music. If you tell him this, he says, 'All students who come to me are sent to me by God, so whatever I teach and they learn is destined to be given to them through me by God.'

During one of our conversations for this book, I asked him how he managed to stick with it, against the odds, through times that were undeniably hard, without getting tired, disappointed or losing hope. He considered my question silently for a while and said, 'When you really need to do something, or your desire for something is very great and very important to you, you find a way to do it. Most people are like that, it is just that some people do not always know what it is they need to do, and what they desire. Life and people around you can distract you from your purpose, or confuse you about your purpose. This is the difficulty.' I was digesting this, admitting to myself the truth of it, when he continued. 'Beta, I was never in the "race". The race that the world tries to make you think is your reason for living. I was never competing with anybody. I never tried to show anyone down so that I could look good; I only followed the path of my music with pure dedication. Had I been in the race, I would have gotten tired and would never have been able to get here. I never wanted to defeat anybody, but just improve myself. I had no rival, enemy or competitor; I only had to work on myself. My life is my music and my riyaz.'

Living the life of an 'ustad' was not easy. There was great effort, sacrifice and determination needed, and a self-discipline that many of us aspire to develop in ourselves. This is why he is not an ordinary man. It is his philosophy and his practice, the way he lives and breathes each moment. This is how he achieves his dreams. The boy who ran away from his house to live a dream, then returned to the responsibilities of working to achieve his dream, the young man who travelled and experienced so many new and different things, people, cultures, music. His life is about learning, sharing knowledge, and supporting and encouraging others to do the same.

I feel like a channel between him and you, grateful that I am able to bring his story to you. As I write this, knowing in my heart that I have tried to tell his story truthfully and honestly, I am aware that there is so much more to the man that remains known to him alone. Just the fact that his generous affection and trust are showered upon me, blessings in themselves, moves me tremendously. I feel enormous responsibility that I should do justice not only to his life and his achievements, but to the faith he has shown in me. I have tried to be a sutradhar (narrator) to fill in the gaps where I could not have presented the story in his own words, because it is based on the recollections and feelings of his family as well.

If you feel my inadequacy in this task, as I have sometimes felt while undertaking it, forgive me. Though I have tried to bring to you many facets of his life, I still feel there is so much more that he has kept to himself. He is like an ocean that can envelop anything, but nothing can envelop it. His quest for perfection in music is endless. I feel that deep inside him is another story that he keeps hidden from the world. A dream that he has lived all his life . . . A dream I lived alone.

Acknowledgements

To all those I have known at various times of my life, who have taught me, loved me, supported my efforts, and those who did not, due to whom I learnt so much more; those who have chosen me to teach them, honoured my work and me—thank you.

My family, my dear wife Amina, my children and grandchildren—each of you holds a special place in my heart.

Namrata, were it not for you, I would perhaps never have attempted this. I thank you.

My gratitude to Almighty God, because all that I am and all that I receive, these are your blessings.

Ghulam Mustafa Khan

First, I want to thank my literary agents, Suhail Mathur, and Sanjeev Mathur of the Book Bakers Literary Agency for their help in shaping this book and finding the best publisher for it.

A huge thanks to the team at Penguin Random House and my commissioning editor, Milee Ashwarya, for her able guidance in helping turn this dream into reality.

Thanks also to my friend Vishnu Shankar, for motivating me to work with Ustad Ghulam Mustafa Khan on his autobiography.

My hubby, Rabbani Mustafa Khan, for your constant love and support and for believing in me.

To all my family members, on all sides, for your patience with me as this work brewed and bubbled over such a long period.

Dear Ammi, I specially mention you, for your love and affection, and for digging out so many stories that you hold so carefully in your memory.

Murtuza Mustafa, Anuraadha Tewari, Shikha Aleya— each of you has patiently walked with me through a challenging endeavour. There are many others—your support stays in our hearts, and you are all an integral part of this effort.

Most importantly, I acknowledge you, Papa, (or as the world knows you) Ustad Ghulam Mustafa Khan, the most affectionate, honest person I know. Your self-effacing modesty was my biggest challenge through this process. Thank you for letting me work on the story of your life with you.

Namrata Gupta Khan